THE HIS

WATERLOO STATION

By John Fareham

This book is dedicated to my Father who
endured his years of commuting to Waterloo, on a service posting
he hated, so we could have a good life and through that taught me the
meaning of stoicism.
Also to my good school-friends: Christopher Dodds, Michael Cash, Neil
Jackson, Stuart Scott, and Thomas White all of whom joined in
youthful escapes up to the metropolis via Waterloo. I shall not name
which helped me get my first (un-named) newspaper article when a local
cllr (rightly)
said of some pupils "they just clock on" and then nipped up to Town on
the first off-peak.

To AMS the first girl I regularly used Waterloo to go and meet (so much
better than Fenchurch Street), and Shirley Brown - we should have.

Bretwalda Books
Unit 8, Fir Tree Close, Epsom,
Surrey KT17 3LD

info@BretwaldaBooks.com
Website - www.BretwaldaBooks.com
Twitter - @Bretwaldabooks
Facebook - Bretwalda Books
Blog - bretwaldabooks.blogspot.co.uk/ First Published 2013

ISBN 978-1-909099-72-2

Bretwalda Books Ltd

CONTENTS

INTRODUCTION

My railway life covers all four of the Post-Grouping, or their constituent, companies. It may seem odd for the Great-Grandson of a GNR loco-man, and someone who drove as his first engine a preserved Stanier Black Five of the LMS (forgive me Ashton, and thank you to the Draper family), and of whom family legend has it was conceived on the former GWR line, to write about a station built by the L&SWR but Waterloo was the first station I commuted to for both pleasure and work and still remains just ahead of Kings Cross for that. I grew up in Air Force bases forever moving around until finally we ended up in Bracknell – the common features to all "homes" were train-sets

Platforms 1 to 4 seen in the summer of 1914. Note the profusion of straw boaters and the single soldier.

(father and I), a plethora of railway books ever growing, and the inestimable value to be found in the outpourings of the legendary Ian Allen magazines which were handed to me once father finished.

Thomas Hobbes wrote, in, Behemoth, "London, you know, has a great Belly, but no palate, nor taste of right or wrong" and as a young boy passing over the enormous multitude of tracks at Clapham Junction in an over-crowded "off-peak" train I used to think Waterloo was a metaphor for that: ate people in the morning before spewing them all out in an evening. I never managed to write a poem around that metaphor but I have always been fascinated by railway stations and even more so the great termini of the world, so maybe this book will excoriate the memory of my youthful failure as a lovvie.

What is it about stations and most especially termini that so captures the imagination and soul? For me seeing the vast swirling multitudes, diverse as individuals but united in a common moment of travel before pursuing their diverse lives. Stations, full of lovers parting and reuniting, the workers grimly remembering when they were lovers and now earning the wages for "love's young dream" to continue, whilst their excited children get ready for big adventures. Termini are generally huge buildings, with their own different histories, reflecting the passions of those who built and designed in the glorious heyday of railway travel. Characters like Brunel and Stephenson, Brassey and Peto, people who built for longer than they ever imagined – ending in an era of corporate stultifying penny-pinching where if a wholly new station is ever opened it is more likely to be a bus shelter on a featureless platform. Amazingly we still live on Victorian capital, almost as effective and salutary counter-point to those who dismiss the "failures" of Victorian railway building as Beeching was to be later an example of why the State is not an infallible repository of railway wisdom.

The railway industry at birth made a lot of it up as it went along. It has become fashionable to criticise the illogicalities of the British railway network and argue that there should have been greater State planning. Ignoring the questionable belief that the State is either the font of all wisdom or that it is desirable for State planning the simple fact remains that in the early Nineteenth Century the state did not have either the capacity or the knowledge to plan railways. Central planning was the option for those countries that followed in our wake largely relying on British expertise, an expertise gleaned from having the freedom to try – and to fail.

As a result of being pioneering and trailblazing much of the language used was, as is the British way, largely adapted and sometimes contrived. With a knowledge built on roads and canals some of the terminology was borrowed – what we now think of as an Americanism, "the railroad", was far from atypical in England and so the term "approach roads" was (and still is) often used to describe the route the tracks take to somewhere specific like a station or marshalling yard. As a result if one line bifurcated into two lines separated by a single platform in a station the term "approach road" was in use to describe the single track it then not being untypical to refer to the bifurcated tracks as "platform lines".

This leads to the vexed terminology for "platform", itself sometimes called a "stage" in the early years. We have grown used to the phrase meaning the point at which we shift between train and terra firma but it was not always so. Strictly speaking, in architectural terms, the platform is the entire timber/concrete stage – the actual structure. So a single "stage" could in fact comprise two "platforms" if it has a track on either side of it – one platform could have two platform faces but be numbered as "One" if the railway preferred numbering the structure, or "one" and "two" if they numbered where you could board a train.

So, for example the new Waterloo, as we will see, had 21 "platforms" being the points at which people could get on a different train – but only 13 platforms were actually built – eight of them were double sided.

This has led to much confusion when researching amongst various secondary sources as they have used terms differently, sometimes even in the same work, and the L&SWR were just anarchic about platforms before they started to build the new Waterloo Station at the end of the Nineteenth Century. Primary sources were also often imprecise, to modern eyes, in what terminology was being used. I very much hope I have not added to this confusion.

No history can ever be "definitive" – there are always new facts to be found and the orthodoxies of today could be rewritten in five minutes or a generation. Equally vexing for historians are corporate mergers and wars, or outsourcing municipal service and loss of archival materials, all can cause the loss of archival sources, their information either lost or only to be gleaned from the use made by others but only to be found in secondary sources and all the risks that may imply. Primary sources are not always reliable (the printed souvenir of the station opening records it being opened by the King for example, and memoirs can be self-serving or indeed simple errors of recall), nor is the Historian's interpretation always correct. Indeed the historian's selection, or rejection, of facts can shape the interpretation of the facts as can the presentation which can be challenged by other historians.

In writing a history of a station and the affairs of a railway in so far as they relate to that station over a period of more than 150 years I have researched extensively but like anyone else cannot claim exhaustively. I rejected much material myself (it would have been good, for example to explore more of the conjectural proposals around Waterloo and while reference was made to some hare-brained schemes that impacted on Waterloo directly it would have been interesting to reflect on the LCC's plans for Charing Cross/Lion Brewery and the knock-on effect that might have impacted on Waterloo), and the editor will have to make rejections to the script sent for commercial considerations. It is hoped that none of those rejections will spoil bits people are looking for and enjoy. Equally I hope that, where primary sources seem incomplete, and I have had to rely on secondary sources which are often contradictory, the balance of probability I have taken is sustainable. Those who have helped me in this, and all other matters, are in the acknowledgements although as ever, in the phrase no less true because it is a hackneyed cliché, all responsibility is mine.

CHAPTER ONE

The march to Waterloo (Bridge)

"As long as I gaze on Waterloo sunset, I am in Paradise"

Ray Davies sang in 1967 but it was unlikely anyone would have thought that a century earlier in 1867. Victorian Waterloo Bridge was a monument to laissez-faire Victorian railway planning and bore no recognition to an ordered station, lacking the small matter of sequential platform numbering or indeed much sense of order at all.

What we now call Waterloo Station was first built and opened by the London and South Western Railway (henceforth L&SWR or "the Company") as Waterloo Bridge Station in 1848, the first official use being on 11th July. Before being officially adopted Waterloo Bridge Station by name the station was also known as "York Road", after the nearby road, and referred to as such in Acts of Parliament. Although the L&SWR still aspired to reach the City of London, where many suburban short-haul passengers worked, Waterloo Bridge was nearer The City than the original terminus for the railway company which was at Nine Elms. To understand Waterloo it is important to understand the decisions made at the first terminus at Nine Elms

Nine Elms was a four-acre site, originally selected because it could be approached with little interference to property, described at the time as "a low and marshy place studded with windmills and pollard trees and Dutch-like in appearance". Nine Elms was located near the Vauxhall end of Nine Elms Lane, in the Parish of Battersea and the County of Surrey, just south of Vauxhall Bridge located close to a river pier vital to allow passengers to reach other parts of London. Whilst not significantly further from the commercial heart of London than Paddington (built1838) and Euston (1837), and a mile closer to the retail areas of London than Paddington Nine Elms was not as

The famous Victory Arch is often thought to be the main entrance, but officially is only a side pedestrian access.

close to the City as London Bridge (1836) which was also on the southern side of the Thames despite the City, in those days, being entirely on the North Bank.

In a trial run to Woking, from Nine Elms, a top speed of 25mph was achieved on the first trip, 12th May 1838. Following second trials, on 19th May the line was opened to the public, with no ceremony, on 21st May 1838 with a service based on five trains each way every day.

Whilst Nine Elms as a passenger station had been convenient for a steam ferry to the City (leaving from Old Swan Pier on Upper Thames Street), and a horse-drawn omnibus connection to assorted parts of London, it also had some modest freight use. Nine Elms was also convenient for freight barges, the railway owning ¾ acre for a freight yard which was accessed by a single track, over Nine Elms Lane worked by horses. However the site, being part of Lambeth Marsh was not at the heart of the City itself or the West End.

The London and South Western Railway, owner of both Nine Elms and Waterloo Bridge, was first publicly promoted in a prospectus on 6th April 1831 as the Southampton, London and Branch Railway and Dock Company where the "branch" was to be Basingstoke to Bath and Bristol. The railway was ultimately promoted as the London and Southampton Railway, having dropped the branch proposals, obtaining Parliamentary approval on 25 July 1834. It was Southampton's emergence as a more desirable Channel port than Dover or Portsmouth that meant a railway for the full London to Southampton length became a more viable project. Nevertheless, presaging an intermittent trend throughout the Company's history, organisation of the railway building was chaotic and a firm grip did not start until the appointment of Joseph Locke as engineer in 1837, with Locke dismissing multiple contractors and only retaining Thomas Brassey who proceeded with the dash and verve that would lead him to the top of his profession. Locke's dynamism harnessed with that of W.J. Chaplin, the former substantial road haulier of Chaplin and Horne who sold his interests and invested in the modernity of trains becoming a L&SWR Director and rising to be Chairman in 1843, was an early forerunner of the later focus and dynamism between Herbert Walker and Hugh Drummond.

As we have seen the London and Southampton was an early entrant in what became the lucrative London suburban passenger market but it also aspired to capture Portsmouth traffic. The aspiration to reach Portsmouth, and an awareness of civic pride, prompted the Company to obtain a name change, as part of the Parliamentary powers for the Portsmouth line (which it eventually reached on its own metals on 24th January 1859). The Company's newest Act succeeded on 4th June 1839; an Act which, under Section 2, also officially changed the name to the London and South Western Railway. The L&SWR reached Southampton in 1840 with an inaugural run on 11th May 1840, departing at 8am from Nine

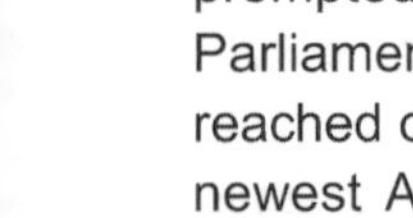

Elms, behind the locomotive "Venus", reaching Southampton three hours later.

Despite the railway starting out in the "inter-city" market it is important not to underestimate the importance of the shorter journeys that together made up the run to Southampton and, eventually, other major population centres on the long-haul runs because even by 1840 the short haul passenger market was lucrative for the L&SWR revenues. The original section of the railway, between Nine Elms and Woking, had intermediate stations at Wandsworth (later renamed Clapham, but closed when the current Clapham Junction was opened), Wimbledon, Kingston (originally to the west of Ewell Road Bridge but moved to reflect popular demand) and now known as Surbiton, Esher (then known as Ditton Marsh), Walton, and Weybridge, and had run them profitably. The L&SWR became even more commuter orientated when the new branch line, initially promoted by an independent concern, from Richmond to what is now known as Clapham Junction opened on the 27th July 1846. With intermediate stops at Wandsworth, Putney, Barnes, and Mortlake the Richmond to Clapham junction line swiftly generated almost a quarter of all London commuter traffic – and was later extended to Reading and Windsor (1st December 1849) in Royal Berkshire causing those railway lines thenceforth to be referred to, within the Company, as "the Windsor Lines".

An independent company promoted the Richmond Railway (eventually opened in 1846) taking a route north of the L&SWR as far as Nine Elms and crossing the L&SWR line near Nine Elms, then proceeding to a point adjacent to Hungerford and Waterloo Bridges, termed the "West End" despite being nowhere near the fashionable "west end" shopping district which, in any event, was located on the northern side of the Thames. When, in 1844, the L&SWR took over promotion of that part of the Richmond line from Nine Elms to Waterloo they also accepted a newer station was desirable, and that same year they began buying land. Parliamentary powers were eventually obtained on 31st July 1845 for an extension to York Road near the southern end of Waterloo Bridge; no less an authority than

Robert Stephenson telling the Royal Commission on Metropolitan Railway Termini, established in April 1846, that there was no site south of the river better suited for a station. Joseph Locke however pointed out to the Royal Commission that despite the railway being swifter some business traffic still preferred the coaches between Chertsey and the City. Clearly with an eye on future expansion Chaplin told the Royal Commission, which reported on 27th June 1846, that despite being located on a 10 acre site Waterloo Bridge Station was inadequate for handling goods traffic. Chaplin argued Waterloo was handicapped because the new Lion Brewery, designed by Francis Edwards and built in 1836-37 for James Goding, obstructed access to the river.

The L&SWR did not intend Waterloo Bridge to be their London terminus. Already active in the commuter market the Company wished to cross the Thames and get their passengers directly into the City. Acquiring another Parliamentary Act on 26th August 1846, and even buying some land, the Directors of the Company now had the powers and the property to extend the line to a terminus just

A 4-6-0 locomotive hauls a passenger train out of Waterloo in 1922, the year the new station opened.

south-west of London Bridge right on the edge of "the City" and build a terminus they intended to share with the North Kent Railway. Long-term plans not withstanding work on the new extension towards Waterloo Bridge was begun in the summer of 1846, with Locke as the engineer and Tite as the architect, although his talents were not to be put to extensive use.

On 2nd July 1847 the L&SWR acquired a Supplementary Act of Parliament for more land at the Waterloo Bridge site and more approaches to service the station. The sum of L&SWR powers conferred by Parliament allowed theoretical expansion towards a more central metropolitan location near the City which had an intermediate station at Vauxhall and allowed for a short branch to Hungerford Bridge. The L&SWR exertions with Parliament thereby empowered them to deliver both goals for their pedestrian traffic – closer to the City and closer to the West End.

Originally projected to cost the far from mean sum of £800,000 Charles Lee, who was the valuer and surveyor for the L&SWR, later admitted the extension cost nearer £1,250,000 which was almost a quarter of the Company's market capitalisation in 1849. The expansion programme was aided by the generous financial powers of the era which, in the original London and Southampton Act of 1834, authorised the Company to raise £1 million in 20,000 shares of £50, and allowed the Company to borrow in excess of 1/3 of its authorised share capital. Additionally the L&SWR was statutorily allowed to borrow up to half the authorised share capital through mortgaging the remainder of the instalments on the shares when half of the calls had been made. A further flotation in 1837 had empowered further capital stock of £400,000 with a loan of £139,000.

Nor had "Railway Mania" collapsed and so the expansion costs were digestible by a company facing increasing traffic and commercially competitive premises but are factors that need to be borne in mind when considering later development was piece-meal and that nothing comprehensive about the station was to be done until some two generations later. It may also be argued that the fact the land the railway advanced over was almost entirely owned by the

Bishops of Winchester, Rochester, and London along with the Archbishop of Canterbury aided the completion of the task. The Church, either through ambiguity about the uses put to their land or indeed perhaps from a wish to benefit from the railway boom themselves, offered no opposition to expanding the line. Despite the need for negotiations involving 1,600 parcels of land containing cottages, coach sheds, hop warehouses et al the Church as the dominant landowner in the area had allowed large holdings in relatively few hands which streamlined negotiations.

Landowner resistance had increased the delay and expense suffered by other railways to the east and north-east of London – a city in which something like 800 acres of central land in the 19th Century were acquired for railway uses although they were expressly forbidden from penetrating the geographic central region as defined by Parliament.

The new Waterloo Bridge Station was officially opened to the public on 11th July 1848, the day after Nine Elms closed for passenger traffic. The first train to arrive at Waterloo Bridge was the Southampton mail- train which, drawn by "Hornet", arrived at the new terminus at 4.30 am bringing some 40 passengers on 11th July 1848. It is not clear if Hornet itself arrived because at that time trains often arrived into London termini under rope-hauled traction not at all an atypical practice of the era and one which only ceased at Waterloo in 1866. However the service started and although there was theoretical provision for further extension of the line towards the City at London Bridge that seemed to be the extent of the railway company's planning – the station itself was a completely uncoordinated affair and initially no proper station buildings were actually built. The Chairman of the Company perhaps showed the priorities when he reported "We have placed on the railway four distinct lines that we may have no troubles or inconveniences in future in the traffic."

The new station at Waterloo Bridge had a width of 280' and occupied some 3/4 acre, approximately covering the area currently occupied by Platforms 7 to 12, being built some 20' above street level on yet more arches. With considerable foresight 10 acres of land containing agricultural buildings and parts of eight streets, not all of which was initially to be used, had been acquired by the Company.

The iron platform roof was of two 140' spans covering all six tracks, two of which were centre roads for marshalling stock. Accounts now vary on how many platforms there were: the L&SWR in their centenary claiming three platforms with no clarity about their terminology and Jackson claims four platforms with six faces. More recently the South Western Circle, a group of enthusiasts about the L&SWR, make a compelling case the four tracks not used for marshalling served a two platform configuration both of which only had a single face, with departure on the east and an arrival platform on the west. Because each single platform face served two railway lines both platforms served two tracks broadly running end to end on each platform. In light of the desire to push on to the heart of London, and the experiences of Nine Elms with its layout and buildings the case is compelling indeed as it would have enabled a simple, low-cost, forward progression that would have left Waterloo Bridge as a conventional interim line-side station. What is more generally agreed on is initially 300' long each platform doubled in length quite soon after opening and actually ran on an axis broadly north to south, despite the L&SWR heroically referring to both sides of the track (and all subsequent extensions) as "North" and "South". The actual orientation of the station clearly showed the intended expansion towards the City because of which it was initially designed and built as a through station, ensuring no buildings were located at the end of the lines the tracks merely running up to the end wall in Waterloo Road. Having vehicle ramps either side of the station with, on the east, an approach taken, at a slope, off the then York Street (now Leake Street) – the exit being into Waterloo Road where the station's main entrance was located. However the Headquarters of the railway was located at the new station from the beginning of its existence.

The station frontage itself also gave a road access with a cab yard. The road access was up from York Road via a tunnel from Griffin

Street, and down via another ramp into Waterloo Road; a similar arrangement replicated this layout for the arrival platforms. It is not entirely clear from surviving records when the frontage on to Waterloo Road was built. Built in the classical style with three arches of two disparate sizes (a wide one with narrower on each side) at platform level, the pediment contained the "South Western Railway" in large lettering alongside each angle. With more room on the street level plinth the Company put "London and South Western Railway". However it is not unreasonable to posit that, with the railway mania ending and creation of an Enlargement Committee, the railway would want to present a good "shop front" to the Waterloo Road

Meanwhile on the eastern side of the railway approach roads to Waterloo Bridge Station a separate and private station owned by the London Necropolis and National Mausoleum Company (LNNMC) was completed in October 1854, built solely for transporting the dead of London to the new Brookwood Cemetery near Woking. Arrangements for the dead needed careful and sensitive handling since, by 1858, Waterloo Bridge Station handled some four million passengers a year. Discretion over the deceased was met by placing the Necropolis Station away from the main station in a site bounded by Westminster Bridge Road to the south, and York Street on the north. The down line of the L&SWR, and the backs of various houses and shops respectively set the western and eastern boundaries to Necropolis. The Necropolis building, which cost £23,231/14/4, was three storeys high at the main part the third storey being at the height of the railway line, with its main entrance a variegated brick archway from Westminster Bridge Road, being exited by an archway to York Street, this archway being generally treated as the secondary one. The platform building was designed by Tite with the assistance of Sir William Cubitt. Necropolis Station had two short sidings and a single platform with quite a modest building connected by a stairway to their office, converted houses formerly 1 to 3 Church Street in York Street, opposite All Saints Church.

In 1855 a Parliamentary "Select Committee on Metropolitan Communications" was looking into the traffic chaos engulfing London

The Queen welcomes Prime Ministers in 1960, by which date trains were being used less for official functions.

and the L&SWR again shewed no attachment to Waterloo as the end of the line. During the Commission hearings, plans were submitted by the L&SWR to extend the line from Waterloo towards the West End crossing the Thames to Hungerford food market. By demolishing the toll levying, pedestrian only, Hungerford Bridge and replacing it with a much larger railway bridge a sizeable reduction in road traffic across Westminster and London Bridges was expected. The proposed terminus station on the bridge would have had entrances on both sides of the river, and a pedestrian pathway along the sides, but the scheme was not encouraged by the Commission.

Undaunted the L&SWR looked at other methods of getting their customers to both the City and the West End. In the spring and summer of 1859, an independent railway company successfully promoted a Bill which meant in that year Parliament passed An Act for the making and maintaining of the Charing Cross Railway, and for other Purposes (Henceforth the Charing Cross Railway Act) authorising the extension towards Charing Cross, from London

Bridge. The L&SWR had proposed inserting clauses in the Bill allowing the building of a connection from Waterloo towards Charing Cross thereby giving them an option of "constructing a Branch Line to join the Charing Cross Line near the South bank of the River Thames, and of running over the river on the Charing Cross line and using the Charing Cross Station, and if that option was exercised the South Western should pay £200.000 for the accommodation to be provided for them". The matter of tolls would be settled by arbitration. The L&SWR proposal was rejected whereupon the L&SWR were unsuccessfully invited to become shareholders in the entire undertaking of the Charing Cross Railway line.

The Charing Cross Railway Act of 1859 nevertheless contained Section 36 requiring a connection between the two lines namely, "The Company shall not open or use for traffic the Railway without at the same time opening for traffic the Branch Railway"

With the increasing recognition that, in the main, Waterloo Bridge was now likely to be "the end of the line" in terms of station buildings, and in any event being the subject of extensive public criticism, the L&SWR took an objective look at its terminus with its manifest shortcomings. The Waterloo Station Enlargement Committee, created in 1859, reported that improvement works could be undertaken for £42,000, and specifically kept open the option to continue the line. The new "North Station", often informally known as the "Windsor Station" was geographically located towards the north-western side of the Waterloo Bridge station and extended the terminus to the approximate position of the current Platform 16. Opened on 3rd August 1860, with two arrival and two departure lines three platforms were built at Windsor Station with the centre platform having a track on each side, and it also allowed an additional ticket platform for the up main line to be established between the up main line and the down Windsor Line betwixt Westminster Bridge Road and Church Street Road; and to the westernmost side of the site, again learning from the Nine Elms experience, a rail spur pointed towards the Thames. The usual gap between adjacent lines of railway at this time was 6' but this ticket platform was some 2 ½" deficient of that space meaning an iron rail was erected 2' from the southernmost rail of the Windsor down line which stood 4' 10"above the railway tracks, to protect the ticket collector. The unsatisfactory platform arrangement was roundly condemned by Colonel Yolland in his Report on the death of James Adams which happened two weeks after an accident on 8th September 1860 when the rail was caught by an open door snapped off and impaled Adams in the leg.

The Windsor Station acquired its own booking office and waiting rooms, as well as a passenger concourse behind the buffers, but also played host to the whole ensemble's main parcel office despite being physically separated from the "Main Station" by a cab yard accessed from both York and Waterloo Roads. However some operational cohesion was maintained by the use of a dock siding in the Main Station for Windsor Line operational purposes.

In 1861 Parliament authorised the construction of the Cannon Street Branch and Station from the Charing Cross line and, in August 1861, the L&SWR and SER held discussions to see if any arrangement was possible to give the L&SWR access to Cannon Street. The SER opinion was the L&SWR would reap very great advantages possessing a station in the City, and SER interests would be prejudiced thereby but, despite a proposed scheme which was thought likely to be agreeable to the SER being put to the L&SWR Board in October 1861, the Board finally declined to authorise further discussions in November. At this period Waterloo Bridge was handling some 228 passenger trains a day so was indeed generating traffic which wanted to move to different points in the metropolis.

With opening of the new line being imminent the L&SWR had become concerned enough to write to the SER, who had been allowed to amalgamate with the "independent" railway, about their perception they would be left out in the cold. Samuel Smiles, author of books such as "Self Help", but also the Secretary to the SER, replied, in April 1863, they, "will take care to observe the provision contained in Clause XXXVI of the Act to the effect that the company not open the line for traffic without at the same time opening the Branch line abutting on your Station... [and that the]... Directors have

Elizabeth Taylor and Richard Burton were regulars at Waterloo, catching the Cunard boat train to Southamtpon.

not yet thought it necessary to make arrangements for the working of the traffic, but ...that when the proper time comes they will be prepared to submit every detail in the arrangement which may involve the use of any part of your station ... for...approval in writing, as provided by Clauses XXXIV of the Act." The line from London Bridge to Charing Cross opened on Monday 11th January 1864, and the Bills announcing the opening stated, inter alia, that, "The London Bridge and Waterloo Train services will commence on Monday 1 February." Accordingly correspondence took place in January and February 1864 between the two railway companies over whether compliance had been made with Section 36 of the Act.

To give L&SWR means to get to Cannon Street meant, in 1864, a single line connection was punched through the front of Waterloo

Bridge Station. With characteristic Victorian "go-ahead" exuberance, and having no regard to the architectural aestheticism of the existing frontage, the new 5 chain long (there are 80 chains to a mile) line extended what had hitherto been a siding between Platforms 2 and 3. Crossing the concourse of the L&SWR terminus the new line exited what had previously been the front wall of their station, well above street level. The new line crossed over the Waterloo Road by a bridge and connected to the SER train line by forming a junction facing London Bridge just at the point the SER line passed the east end of Waterloo Bridge Station. Built by the SER, famously described by Nock as resembling "a horizontal jet of water from the mouth of a gargoyle" (showing go ahead architecture and gargoyles can co-exist if not very harmoniously), this also meant the SER could advertise their services and station directly from L&SWR property!

On 17th December 1864, and stressing how many shareholders the two companies had in common, the L&SWR wrote to the SER pushing for the erection of a station to aid passengers using the connecting line . Smiles replied on 12th January 1865,

"Although it would doubtless be possible to construct a station at the point indicated by you, this Company does not possess the legal powers of purchasing the property requisite for the purpose; and my Directors doubt whether a Station worked in the manner indicated by you would conduce to the convenience of the travelling public.

My Directors regret that the service of trains which it was proposed to run between Kensington Station and London Bridge, and to which the London and North Western Company and this company were agreeable, has not been tried by your Company. On this and any other subject my Directors will be happy to meet a deputation of your Board."

In agreeing to a meeting the L&SWR made clear their view it was impracticable to carry through Waterloo Bridge a train service between London Bridge & Kensington. Following the works so recently undertaken at Waterloo Bridge the Directors advised,"...the attempt to do so would involve the entire reconstruction of the Waterloo Station at a very large cost, and they are convinced that they would not be justified in incurring such a cost for so small an advantage to either Co. or to the public…".

Connections to Waterloo Bridge were not always above ground. Waterloo Bridge's first tube proposal came in 1865 when the Waterloo and Whitehall Railway Company received Parliamentary approval, on 5th July 1865, for a ¾ mile route from the Whitehall end of Great Scotland Yard to a point adjacent to the arches of Waterloo Station. The underground proposed was to be a pneumatic railway relying on a 12' 9" diameter cast-iron tube in 200' lengths and riveted together which would pass through the Thames, the tubes resting on four brick piers sunk into the river bed. Although some works were started, and £70,000 expended there were not enough funds and work ceased in 1868, the Parliamentary powers lapsed in 1871, and the company was finally dissolved in 1882, with the Parliamentary Act included for repeal, along with some 800 others, in an unopposed second reading in the House of Lords on 5th November 2012. A pneumatic railway or not, it shewed that others also thought there was traffic to be generated in crossing from one side of the Thames to the other, although the L&SWR gave no active support to the Waterloo and Whitehall Railway Company proposal, despite having two Directors in common. The aborted works were not wasted - they later became the wine cellars of the National Liberal Club!

If the tube was not arriving at Waterloo Bridge Station the existing passenger growth meant serving the increasing multiplicity of lines, and increasing train volumes now at some 228 passenger trains a day around the early 1860s, required a newer approach to signalling so the points and signals on the approach to the terminus were concentrated into the first "A" signal box in March 1867 built by Messrs Stevens & Sons. Constructed on a gantry some 200 yards to the south of Waterloo Station or 75 yards from the extreme end of the platforms, and proximate to Necropolis, spanning over all four approach roads the A box housed a 47 lever locking-frame with 24 designated for the main-line movements and 23 for the Windsor lines the frames arranged in two rows parallel to the railway. Handling some 400 trains a day the 1867 box was distinguished by two masts each carrying three pairs of back-to-back semaphore signals where each pair was linked by a single pivot in a classic style originally erected by Charles Hutton Gregory on the London and Croydon Railway.

An interesting operational point pre-1869 was the dependency of the terminus on the Vauxhall Station. In keeping with their quite laissez-faire approach to so many matters, Waterloo was an early example of an "open station" in the sense that those neither on railway business or travelling were also allowed on premises and platforms, thereby, inter alia, giving opportunities for fraudulent travel. To combat fraud trains stopped outside the terminus allowing tickets to be collected by railway staff however, with over 200 trains a day, this was not the most efficient operating practice and in 1869 the halt was shifted back to Vauxhall for two minutes during which time an extensive number of clerks were employed to check and collect tickets. Amazingly this co-dependency between Waterloo and Vauxhall in terms of passenger bona-fides continued to varying degrees until 1916 - finally extinguished by the increased introduction of corridor coaches and the new Waterloo Station having platforms equipped with ticket barriers.

1869 also saw the L&SWR start to provide a train connection from Richmond to Waterloo Bridge via Addison Road (now known as Kensington Olympia), a station which the London and North Western Railway (L&NWR) trains would serve from 1872. The Addison Road station, and the arrival of the L&NWR, was the point at which it could be said Waterloo Bridge Station and Euston were connected, although this was not to be regarded as a core service to be kept in time-tables at all costs, or ideal route optimisation and as such largely excluded from this work.

Equally, the actual physical arrangements for passengers using the L&SWR/SER service were not satisfactory in the Blackfriars Road area and therefore the L&SWR continued to press the SER to honour the terms of their Act and build a station. The SER opened the new station, naming it "Waterloo Junction", to the east of the junction on 1st January 1869 patterning it on the Blackfriars Road model which station was itself shut the previous day. Whilst the commuter had the simple physical task of walking across a footbridge over the connecting line and taking an SER train to Charing Cross or Cannon Street (opened by the SER on 1st September 1866 from their London Bridge Charing Cross line) the L&SWR and SER had several issues regarding through booking arrangements, so passenger transfer between Waterloo and the SER's terminus at Cannon Street, vital for the L&SWR's City traffic, remained challenging.

Much simpler for the L&SWR was the steadily growing Windsor Line traffic which meant that the former dock siding of the Main Station was adapted, on 17th March 1869, into a running road with a platform: an operational harmony not replicated in the architecture nor readily comprehensible to the casual passenger.

Suburban traffic was lucrative and continued to grow which meant the decision was taken to relieve the original 1848 station of all local trains to Hampton Court, Kingston, and Epsom as part of a plan to widen the approaches and add more platforms to the Waterloo ensemble. The L&SWR gained Parliamentary approvals in 1874 and 1877 to acquire adjacent land, occupied by narrow streets and packed with houses. The 1867 A box and associated signalling was replaced in 1874 by a Saxby & Farmer box built alongside the original one and equipped with 109 levers in one length, this time at right-angles to the railway, and when all were connected the original A box was removed. The Main A box (the B C D boxes were further from the station and thus not featured in this work) were supplemented by three yard cabins. One yard cabin was on the west side by the turntable near York Road and another was near the end of the South Station platform. There is some controversy around "the Crows Nest" signal box, some saying it dates from the beginning of the station at Waterloo, but as early as 1892 the L&SWR's A. W. Szlumper (of whom more later) clearly stated the 1867 box was the first signal box. Therefore the Crows Nest, built above Central Station against the gable end of the roof there, controlling the station and internal turntables arrived as a "yard cabin" in 1874. None of the yard cabins

The 4-6-0 King Arthur Class locomotive "Tintagel" leaves Waterloo with the Exeter Express in summer 1937.

survived the building of the new station.

Increasing traffic meant the Windsor Line buildings gained a direct vehicular approach from York Road in 1875 with the provision of an access from there that ran parallel to Mepham Street. The suburban services were not the only growth area as the former Kensington through service was partly resumed from 1st July 1875, the L&NWR deciding to run some seven trains a day each way between Willesden Junction, north of Addison Road, and Waterloo – a thirty minute journey.

Parliamentary powers alone were not enough to secure the L&SWR's plans because the presence of Necropolis Station hindered the L&SWR expansion plans. In 1875 therefore the L&SWR made an arrangement to take over the outer line to Necropolis Station, in return they would replace the Necropolis train-shed with a single line one, and the LNNMC gained exclusive ownership of that land hitherto leased from the L&SWR since 1854.

Other localised agreements between the two companies at Waterloo and Necropolis followed in 1876 and 1877 which meant at the end of 1877 the L&SWR obtained the better access to their outer line when they removed the roof and western wall of the Necropolis' private train shed. The LNNMC secured other significant gains during the negotiations including a 999 year lease on their station site, an extended platform as recompense for the lost siding, and a platform awning featuring "The London Necropolis Company" in a narrow valance that faced the L&SWR approach tracks. The awning also had cast-iron cantilever supports with the "LNC" initials in them. The interesting outcome of this work for Necropolis was that the station was more revealed to those using the L&SWR.

The works at Necropolis meant works at Waterloo Bridge could progress and, on 26th September 1878, the L&SWR notified the Board of Trade that, "...the improvements at this station are rapidly approaching completion and are expected to be ready for inspection in one month from this date". The Board of Trade were petitioned on 16th October by the L&SWR to examine the new bridge and other works after which on the following day an Inspector, Major-General Hutchinson RE, was appointed and the Company notified. The inspection duly took place, the works being described by the Inspector as "...where two additional platform lines ...and commodious offices have been obtained". This was in fact a very long single wooden platform of the island type servicing a track to either side, thereby allowing some main-line suburban services, the Epsom and Leatherhead, Hampton Court, and Kingston via Norbiton, to be operated from it, and also allowing the rearrangement of some lines across the ensemble as well as widening and raising the existing platforms. The absence of a running board and therefore the unduly large gap between the carriage and the platform was blamed for the death of the prominent Jewish banker and MP for Reading Sir Francis Goldsmid who had been crushed between a railway carriage and the platform in an accident at Waterloo Station when leaving a moving train, the resultant injuries causing his death at St Thomas's Hospital, Lambeth, on 2nd May 1878. There was no shortage of questions in Parliament as a result of Colonel Yolland's criticisms of the Company, questions asked in both the Commons and the Lords revolving around why there was no running board on the carriage. The reason given for there being no running board was inconsistent platform height across the L&SWR network making running boards on carriages impossible. Whilst the government, and the Company, generally stone-walled to resist legislative interference on the matter of running boards platform height was not a subject that could be wholly ignored even in the absence of Parliamentary compulsion.

The new lines were connected with the main lines near the large signal cabin at the entrance of the station and were altogether 17½ chains in length being carried entirely on a viaduct composed of brick arches with girder bridges, over streets crossed by the railway. On one of the girder bridges, specially strengthened for the purpose, part of the large signal cabin was supported. As a result of station expansion the L&SWR asked Stevens & Sons to replace the 1874 A box. Ingeniously, in 1878, Stevens & Sons without disrupting services supplied 35 extra levers, parallel to and interlocking with the existing 109, by building over and around the existing A box then accessing the new space by demolition of any unneeded walls.

Commenting on the signal arrangements with general approval, save for a few small details, the Inspector noted they were the subject of a separate frame in the existing signal cabin but interlocked with the old ones. It was also noted that a barrier had been ordered, but not yet provided for the lift on the new island platform and that the roof over part of the platform was not yet completed. It was felt that since the barrier and roof could be completed before the expected opening the Board of Trade felt no need to object subject to "compliance and inspection"

Officially known as "South Station" (despite being on the east) or "New Station" the building was dubbed "Cyprus" by the railwaymen because the British had recently annexed Cyprus. However named, the approximate site of South Station is the current Platforms 3 to 6. If a rose by any other name is as sweet this could not be said of the new station. Opened on 16th December 1878 South Station had a frontage, running to the boundary line of the Central Station, supported on iron columns over the footpath and carriageway which was enclosed from Waterloo Road by a low brick wall and iron railings. South Station had its own overall platform roof, a separate concourse from the rest of the complex, also its own booking office and refreshment room which overlooked Waterloo Road. Viewed from Waterloo Road the new extension at first-floor level had five sections between pairs of double columns with the outer two sections each having four windows and the inner three sections having three windows each. The join to the existing frontage, already disfigured by the connecting bridge, was not entirely harmonious. Building South Station had necessitated demolishing Charlotte Street and Henry Place thereby pushing the boundary wall of the station to Aubyn Street locating the station on the other side of the cab yard, beyond the easternmost part of the original 1848 station.

Consequently South Station resembled little more than an annexe only connected with the main station, now operationally known as Central Station, by a covered passageway connecting the concourse on the South Station to the Central Station departure platforms and crossed the incline down towards Waterloo Road, or South Station could also be accessed from an uninspiring stairway from the Waterloo Road. The lack of station cohesion was emphasised by, between the South Station and Platform 1 of the "parent" station, locating a small locomotive shed, turntable and some engine lines at one end; and at the other end a cab approach and an office block which included elements of the general offices in it. The South Station island platform was 750' long of an average 23' width being 2' 6" above the rails the hitherto standard height of 1' 9" being deemed too low, and despite serving two tracks, was not numbered at all! With that overall length the single, unnumbered platform with no numbered faces either, regularly housed two full-length trains either side!

It is believed that the new offices built alongside the main departure platform also date from this period. The offices separated the main line departure platforms and the access road to the cab yard, and their similarity of style to the South Station office buildings suggests the dates were broadly similar. The cab yard was commodious, made of iron and glass on ornate pillars.

CHAPTER TWO

The growth of Waterloo 1880+

The concourse in 1914 when the platforms ended at No. 6. Note the familiar glazed roof also ends at this point.

The building of South Station meant improvements could be made to Central Station allowing platform improvements in width and height, some track rearrangement and signalling additions leading in 1880 to 20 more levers. At this point Waterloo Station still coped with four approach roads – two on the west side serviced the Windsor Lines and the two on the east side were the main lines. These four roads fanned out into thirteen platform lines, 8 to 12 for the Windsor Lines, 1, 13 and 14 were for the main line exclusively, and 3 to 7 were common to both lines; line 2 had been taken out at this point. All tracks were controlled from the A cabin with its 135 signal levers.

In common with many stations Waterloo lighting left much to be desired, the existing lights being inadequate in the cavernous stations of the time. In February 1881 South Station was therefore illuminated by 28 "Brush" electric lights as the first attempt to address this problem.

From the early days at Nine Elms in 1846/7 the L&SWR had had telegraph agreements. On 23rd April 1881 the L&SWR and The Right Honourable Henry Fawcett MP (and successors as Postmaster General) reached agreement "to lay down a pipe or tube for the carrying of telegraph wires" between Waterloo Station and the Clapham Junction Station. Payment was agreed at the rate of £1 a mile "for the actual length of the pipe or tube", payable w.e.f. 1st January 1882, but the agreement also gave the Company the right to erect them. This agreement followed one of 10th July 1868 which gave a way-leave for telegraph poles for the benefit of the Postmaster General, although an indenture of 15th June 1880 had released the Postmaster General from having to pay all the sums due under the initial 10th July 1868 agreement.

In 1882, the year the Waterloo and Whitehall Railway was wound up, another connection to Waterloo was authorised by Parliament. The Charing Cross and Waterloo Railway was authorised from Waterloo to Trafalgar Square, which was to be a shallow "cut and cover" railway that would have run under the Thames in two iron tubes. The line was bored out for some 60' of tunnel under the Embankment and Northumberland Avenue but when the 1884 Bill for a connecting line to Oxford Street and thence to St Martin-le-Grand failed, and financial support was not forthcoming, works towards Waterloo were abandoned in 1885.

However the failures of underground companies did not stop the L&SWR deciding to reduce pressure on the original station by extending the station further to the west. The extension necessitated track and signalling works to create the new "North Station" and the opportunity was also taken, in January 1883, to install 245 Edison electric lights in the new station.

To further cope with growing traffic the Company obtained powers, in 1884, to expand the running roads between Nine Elms and Waterloo from four to six. The extended station itself was opened in stages from 1884 when it began beyond the party wall to the old "Windsor/North" station continuing towards York Road. On 24th February 1885 the L&SWR were able to notify the Board of Trade of their intention to open "certain additional lines and other works & signalling & interlocking arrangements at the Waterloo Bridge Station. The signalling works meant a further expansion of the A box with 65 more levers across the entire station, and the L&SWR's letter was acknowledged on the 26th February after an internal Board of Trade Minute was sent out on the 25th February. The Waterloo A box now comprised 209 levers in two parallel rows.

The Inspector reported on 9th March 1885 that the works should be sanctioned subject to the Company advising and arranging an inspection for the new works.

Three of the six new platform lines on the north side extension were opened on 12th March 1885. Sanctioned for use on 28th April 1885 the Company eventually duly reported on 18th November 1885, received and replied to by the Board of Trade the following day, that they wished an inspection of the new lines. The inspector commented:-

"The two platform lines No's 18 and 19 and the whole of the roofing of the station are now finished, and I can recommend that the use of the completed station may be sanctioned

The old roofs over Griffin Street and York Street have been extended to [carry] the lines into the new part of the station, and the girders in these roofs have ample strength and were satisfactory under test.

Completed in November 1885, the Board of Trade sanctioned the part of the extension of the works to Windsor Station on 1st December 1885. Officially the extended Windsor Station, despite being to the western-most part of the ensemble, was known as the North Station but which the railwaymen promptly named "Khartoum" referencing "Chinese" Gordon's death in Africa ten months earlier – a slang name that stuck rather than "Abyssinia", which was attached

Winston Churchill was frequently used Waterloo when on official business for the government.

at an earlier stage of the expansion. Indeed even in the 1970s there was one elderly railway ticket office clerk at Bracknell who readily responded to requests for tickets to “Khartoum” from certain schoolboys clutching pocket-money in their hands and for whom the exotic nature of life in the metropolis was not enough and had to be made to sound even more of an adventure. (Looking back, it was quite a relief that he did not choose to misunderstand and send us, for I was one of those boys, to the other terminus at Reading instead!).

The “Khartoum” extension consisted of six new platform faces under a roof noticeably higher than that over the rest of the station. The extension included new coaling facilities, some carriage sidings, station offices and a 52’ turntable with platforms numbered 7 to 10. Platform 7 backed onto the 1860 station extension where No 10 was usually known as “the Milk” because in the arches underneath it the milk churns arriving from the West Country were stored before onward delivery to London’s dairies. The realignment of lines

enabled the original lines to Windsor in the 1860 allocations to be re-designated as arrivals for main-line services. The station extension also meant that, in terms of signalling, in the 1880s san average of ten men made around 5 million signalling movements a year, while handling some 700 trains a day.

Covered by a substantial roof, Khartoum station also had more offices behind the concourse. The offices continued, in a separate block, along the roadside down to the York Road and housed the management of the L&SWR as well as the Director's Board Room, in a building that was typical of many Victorian office buildings to be found anywhere. From 1885 onwards Waterloo Station occupied some 15 acres, with 16 platform roads and 18 platform faces comprising six at Central, 10 at North and the two at South according to the Company's official version, although some describe it as "4 at Windsor and 6 in North" a distinction not embraced in this work. However any overview clearly showed the Waterloo terminus was still not cohesive, Hamilton Ellis memorably saying, "the old outfit was getting lumpy like a diseased potato". The lack of cohesion was recognised implicitly when even the L&SWR officially called three sections North, Central, and South, let alone the unofficial soubriquets, but operationally Waterloo was very versatile.

To try and brand the parts of the station with coherent identities was to oversimplify the situation and disguise the reality. Although there were 18 platform faces there were actually only 10 numbered platforms! The discrepancy between the platform numbering and the actual tracks stemmed from the L&SWR favoured practice of numbering the physical platform rather than the faces it presented to tracks – although that was to assume the existence of a number at all since South Station's platform was not numbered. Indeed within the Waterloo ensemble there were two sets of platforms numbered 1 and 2 and with four areas that could be regarded as concourses the confusion within the L&SWR's Waterloo can be readily imagined. Platforms 2 and 3 handled some of Waterloo's key services and were like an alternative universe. Platforms 2 and 3 needed to be physically long enough to handle large numbers of carriages but this impeded passenger flows along the concourse because the platforms almost met the wall screening off the drop to Waterloo Road. The connection to the SER line, running across the Central concourse at ground level, itself impeded passenger flows and was spanned, in an effort to provide a short-cut to Platform 3 and beyond, by a small drawbridge as well as a footbridge opposite the booking office. The booking office, still located on Platform 1 further impeded the flow of passengers.

Furthermore, there were double-sided tracks located between Platforms 1 and 2 as well as between Platforms 3 and 4! Whilst Platform 1 was generally for main-line expresses it was far from atypical that, during the rush hour, a suburban tank engine heading to the Surrey stockbroker belt may precede a main-line express.

In 1886 there was a further extension in office block provision, although office administration in a rather uncharacteristic move towards simplifying matters saw the L&SWR station finally reflect the growing tendency in timetables became officially called: Waterloo. The new office block was built facing the York Road itself and this block, along with the one built the previous year meant displacing some 2,000 people from around 400 houses and the removal of Vine Street from the York Road towards Waterloo Road. To the Waterloo Road Waterloo Station presented a frontage cited at between 900 and 1,000' although this was far from architecturally cohesive and still featured the famous excrescence of the bridge.

In 1889 the L&SWR obtained an agreement with the LNNMC to rest, at the latter's pleasure, one of the supporting girders for the signal box on the Waterloo end of the Necropolis platform. In return Necropolis Station secured a wooden screen to the top of arch number 224, their Westminster Bridge Road entrance; and also the lease of land just to the west of that entrance to erect of new office buildings to be numbered as 188 Westminster Bridge Road.

However, whatever the lack of architectural cohesion, absence of coherent master planning, and questionable spatial awareness Waterloo Station(s) at the end of the 1880s were still handling at least 50,000 passengers a day disgorging themselves from some 700 trains daily, the Lost Property Office handling 23,158 items in 1889. So, at the start of the 1890s, despite the chaotic platform organisation and incoherent architectural form of Waterloo the station conspired to serve more passengers than any other station. That the activities at Waterloo were an enormous undertaking was illustrated in "Titbits" magazine of February 1890. "Titbits" edified its readers with news 15 acre station had four miles of permanent way in the station, the total length of the ten platform structures being 2 ½ miles; and which was used by an average of 720 trains and light engines, 740 omnibuses, and 3,480 cabs/carriages a day. Whilst Waterloo remained a predominantly passenger terminus in London 3,523,432 gallons of milk in some 220,779 milk churns passed annually through the station. The whole complex contained 2,760 gas burners/lights and consumed 47½ million cubic feet of gas annually. Operationally however congestion was now no longer just an issue on the platforms but also on the tracks leading into the station

Despite the justifiable earlier confidence, expressed by Chaplin in 1848, modern levels of traffic meant the Westminster Bridge Road approach tracks formed a considerable bottle-neck, the four approach lines were now not adequate to service the 18 platforms. Once again Necropolis Station inhibited unilateral action and again the L&SWR were effectively held to ransom by the LNNMC. The L&SWR needed modifications to the Necropolis Station entrance on Westminster Bridge Road and agreement was secured for the consideration that the entrance be equally ornamental and that all of the arch walls under the railway were lined in white glazed bricks. The completion of the widening of the rail approach between Nine Elms and Waterloo Station to six approach roads (a second up-line for the main-lines and another down Windsor Line) meant Waterloo was now serviced by one Up Windsor, two Down Windsor, two Up Main, and one Down Main line. Looked at from west to east the six approach lines, being the four original and the two new ones, were worked as: up Windsor, down Windsor, down Windsor, up main, up main, down main. Inclusive of widening and enlarging Vauxhall Station the works cost the L&SWR some £600,000. These works meant the displacement of people from their homes, and in 1890 the L&SWR provided tenements for the displaced Vauxhall residents.

Some attempt at rationalisation in Waterloo also took place because of the approach road track-widening works – not that the passengers would notice! The platform roads were renumbered into a coherent semblance of order, starting from South Station, where old platform road No. 14 became No. 1. However the logic on the tracks was not extended to the platforms for the passengers, who still faced an eclectic mix of single and double-sided platforms numbered up to ten over three stations. Track widening meant extending signalling between Waterloo and Nine Elms so for three days, across May 15th to May 17th 1892, the trains at this busy terminus were moved in and out under the protection of flags and lamps - truly a tribute to the efficiency of the staff who avoided accidents and fatalities.

To handle the new lines required increased signalling arrangements so Messrs Stevens & Sons were called in to build a new A box. It was placed alongside and to the north of the original signal box, the new one was built on girders spanning the Windsor Lines with a gangway spanning the main-lines to carry connections such as signal-wires. The 1892 signal-box, opened between 1st May and 15th May 1892, had 236 levers with a gearing system allowing the work of 350 levers in Stevens & Sons largest undertaking to that date. This signal-box was a two-storey construction, continuing the general pattern to at least some extent of its predecessors, with semaphore signals attached on the station side of the signal-box, to the girders it rested on, and showing above the box itself. The top floor of the 74' x 30' box contained the lever frames (in a room 60' x 30'); a lead-lined battery room, relying as far as possible on the Leclanche battery, (15'x9'4"); a telephone room (4' square); and mess room (13'4" x 9' 6"). The lower floor of the signal-box, 9' 5" below the upper floor, contained all the locking machinery and other related workings. When the approach tracks were further widened as part of the new station works the number of levers in this box was increased to 250 and a further six slides – which because of the special engineering was akin to a total of 410 ordinary levers. The

Photographed in March 1922 this very unusual LSWR locomotive is based on a tank engine with carriage.

centenary publication of the railway later claimed by the time the 1892 box was replaced it had 266 levers + 21 slides for route indicating signals. At the turn of the century Waterloo was handling some 900 trains a day with 24,000 lever movements.

It was clear that Waterloo traffic was so busy, and congestion so great, that a further review of operations was needed. The L&SWR and L&NWR discussed the train service connecting their two companies; and separately, in the 1892 Parliamentary session, a proposal emerged for a new tube line from Waterloo. In January 1893 mutual agreement with the L&NWR discontinued both the train service introduced in 1875 and regular use of the line. Parliamentary approval was gained on 27th July 1893 to build a tube line from near the eastern junction of James Street with Lambeth Lower Marsh at Waterloo; terminating at the eastern end of Queen Victoria Street, close to the Mansion House in the City, this new station to be known as "Bank".

The L&SWR, who still knew many of their passengers wished to progress to the City and were probably wearied by the earlier failures to connect their station to the north bank of the Thames, took direct action in 1894. By backing the Waterloo and City Railway financially and supplying five of the eight Directors, including having Air Wyndham Portal as Chairman of both Boards and the General Manager of the L&SWR as a Director, the L&SWR were able to ensure construction of a short tube link, one mile and 46 chains from Waterloo was begun. The first piling started on 18th June 1894, the original idea to power the line from a station on the south river bank was also speedily rejected in favour of location at Waterloo so any spare capacity could be used to light Waterloo. The L&SWR granted an easement on 5th March 1896 to the Waterloo and City to enable the Tube to be built under their General Offices and under or in certain of the arches of Waterloo Station for a consideration of £1,510 chargeable on the rates and tolls of the Waterloo and City and payable quarterly. The first impact on the L&SWR's Waterloo Station was allowing"…the temporary removal of the dining rooms and kitchen used by the uniform staff and such of the clerical staff of the South Western Company as are not members of the dining Club, and at present located in arches 251 and 252 …" enabling the Waterloo Company to pull down and remove the portion of the Central Pier between those arches. The kitchen and dining room were relocated temporarily to archway 250. It is perhaps worthy of note that staff arrangements were no light matter within the station given that in 1896 the Waterloo Station Superintendent (as the L&SWR termed the Station Manager) had 603 staff under his charge which did not include those employed as Headquarter staff. For this reason many staff messed off-site at places such as Mepham Street – decisions that would ultimately have a future impact on the Surrey Room. Those staff were part of the complex arrangements for handling some 50,000 people a day emerging from 800 daily trains in winter; rising to 80,000 daily in summer delivered by 1,040 trains.

The Waterloo and City was swiftly known as "The Drain" some say because it remains one of the leakiest tube lines on the network (and certainly "The Sump" was provided on the Up line side, about 230 yards to the rear of the Waterloo Up Advanced Starting Signal with the express purpose of "receiving and pumping away any water that may drain from the Tunnels"). Others claim the Waterloo and City just "drains away" commuters to the City. This delightful line is completely unconnected to the rest of the London Underground system, and therefore whilst not under their control for many years only appeared on the official London Underground map as a parallel set of dotted lines. The line makes the diagonal journey under London crossing underneath the Thames just upstream from Blackfriars Bridge. In the open land between the former South Station and Lower Marsh the Waterloo vista had originally allowed sight of the Waterloo & City Railway depot, generating station, and sidings, but the new L&SWR terminus and its necessary approach roads would mean eventually the depot came to be almost entirely removed from view. The Waterloo and City line relied on Westinghouse brakes which, being operated by compressed air, had tanks refilled from a compressor and tank at the Waterloo terminus, reinforcing the relationship between the two companies.

At Waterloo Station, the Waterloo and City line was 40 feet below the rails, or 17 feet below street level. To be a success it had to capture the suburban commuter market arriving at the L&SWR's Waterloo. However Berkshire commuters arriving at Khartoum and Surrey Commuters arriving at South Station had the expanse of Central Station separating them. The Drain was therefore accessed from a connecting tunnel by a combination of slopes and stairs emerging at both the South Station, and the easterly side of Khartoum. The slopes at Waterloo were sufficiently steep and long that it was a standing instruction, "The slopes leading to the Platforms at Waterloo must be regularly sanded". Initially both the stations on the Waterloo and City were rather dark and gloomy affairs with bare brick walls and the platforms were almost Stygian. Perhaps this utilitarianism was understandable for a station which really was intended entirely for a simple commuting function and not part of a wider network with more recognised retail and leisure uses.

Despite the recent opening of the new A box sometimes hand signals were still needed in the loco yard only. Working under hand signals a light engine left the engine shed on 21st August 1896. The engine over-ran the clearance point colliding with a down train just leaving Waterloo and derailing the engine with no serious consequences. The sudden stopping of the down train however caught the light engine that was exiting in its wake by surprise and it could not stop in time thus causing it to run up the back of the down train and injuring five passengers.

Waterloo was not the only station in the area nor the only one to cope with growing need to expand. On 27th October 1896 William Rigby, of 5 Denman Street, London Bridge became the contractor to the South Eastern Railway "…to construct and complete the Charing Cross Viaduct Sutton Street to Waterloo Station widening authorised by the South Eastern Railway Act 1889….". The contract was let for £22,102/7/6 and Rigby sublet the ironwork to Messrs Eastwood Swingler and Co of Derby the arbitrator, as provided for under the Arbitration Act of 1889 in case of dispute, was to be William Pollit General Manager of the Manchester Sheffield and Lincolnshire Railway Company.

The following day the Engineering and Estates Committee of the L&SWR minuted "…With reference to the various suggestions which have been made from time to time for the re-arrangement of Waterloo Station instructions were given to Mr Andrews and Mr Galbraith to bring up a complete plan of the station shewing alternative schemes for its enlargement and improvement"

Meanwhile on 12th May 1897 the L&SWR's Engineering and Estates Committee were not entirely satisfied with the new station proposals and resolved to reconsider after the engineers had consulted with the General Manager.

Being a terminus does not always mean the end of the journey and just as "The Drain" was essential, as had been the ferry in earlier generations, one form of transport for onward travel remained, and remains, ubiquitous in London: the cab. Cabs had been servicing Waterloo passengers for many a generation but Waterloo brought a unique state of affairs into being in their application of the service. Most railway companies licensed cabs individually to ply at their own terminus but in 1897 a policy was agreed where "register for one and use all" applied to all stations - except Waterloo! Waterloo demanded, and obtained, a fee of one penny for any cab using their station which continued until 1907 when Parliament enacted an Act to end company licensing.

CHAPTER THREE

The staff-work for the glory at Waterloo

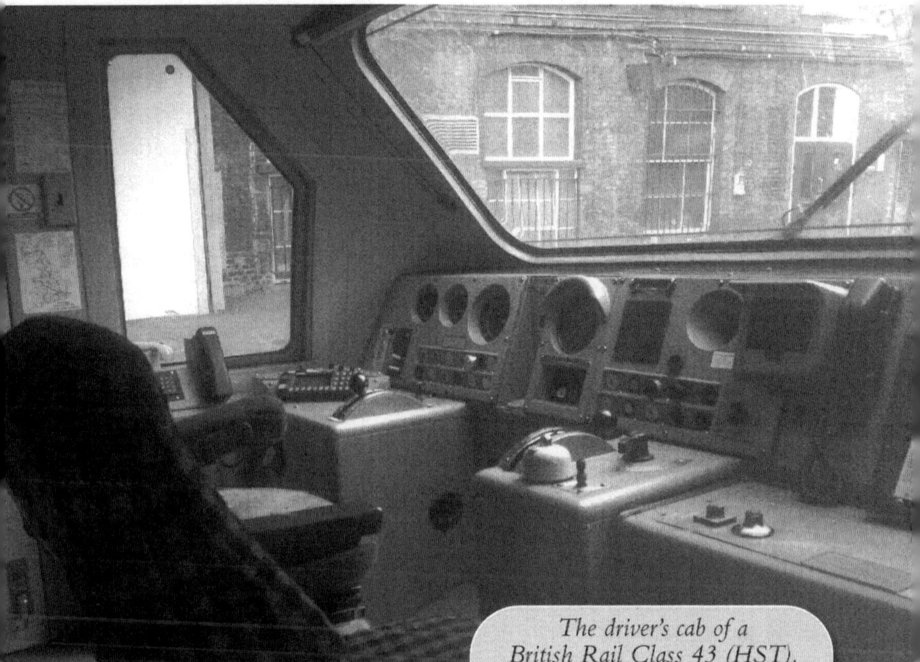

The driver's cab of a British Rail Class 43 (HST). This is the world's fastest diesel train at 148mph.

There was more to occupy the L&SWR however than the ancillary matter of cabs being legislated on by Parliament, their own affairs as part of their core business needed serious overhaul to handle their success. The chaotic situation at Waterloo, so wonderfully parodied in "Three Men in a Boat", could not continue and internal discussions had reached the point the L&SWR promoted a Parliamentary Bill in 1898 to extend the station. The plan was to extend some 6 acres into an area of rather squalid housing beyond the South Station, demolishing Aubyn Street, Griffin Street, York Street, Granby Place, Granby Gardens, Chartley Place and Christie's Place along with the greater part of Launcelot Street and one side of Holmes Terrace. This proposal also necessitated the demolition of All Saint's Church and associated school but it met with such opposition that the Board eventually withdrew the Bill.

The L&SWR Board moved only slowly to the idea of a complete and thorough overhaul of the station and the new Chief Engineer J.W. Jacomb Hood – who deserves to go down in history for his name alone – planned a major reconstruction. Hood, rather radically, went to the United States to look at their latest termini, despite an American writing, in 1886, that on an English railway "...massive stone bridges, the tunnels and viaducts, the station accommodation, and a thousand details of less importance ... combine to produce an impression of solidity and finish, entirely wanting in the majority of American railroads". Hood's original idea was a 23 platform station with a wide passenger concourse, on a new superstructure having a steel-framed frontage block with all the facilities needed. This master-plan was lost in part when economies such as keeping the old Windsor Station roof were eventually decided upon; but whilst two of the proposed platforms were ultimately lost in the execution the rest of the station was eventually built to plan in a large crescent broadly aligned on an east/west axis with tracks entering from a southerly direction.

Initially, at the 9th December 1897 Court of Director's (as Boards were often called in that era) meeting Mr A. Scott, within the architects' section called attention to the accommodation at Waterloo. Scott proposed a general block or ground plan shewing, "a new Main Line Station communicating with the South Station and occupying the space between Aubin Street and the rear of the house properties fronting Lower Marsh with a roadway from the Westminster Bridge and Waterloo Roads" and it was agreed a plan was to be prepared. The Engineering and Estates Committee of 5th January 1898 referred to the Board Minute of the previous December and recorded that "...the engineer submitted plans shewing how this station could be enlarged on the south side between Aubin Street and Lower Marsh" resolving that these plans should be put to the Board.

By 16th March 1898 the Engineering and Estates Committee were able to discuss the Engineer's Report and letter of 14th inst. in which he had been able to submit amended plans and a model. The plans and model were duly submitted to the Court of Directors the following day.

The Court of Directors resolved the matter be reconsidered at their meeting on 31st March 1898 where they resolved "...plan and model therein mentioned were submitted and ordered to come up again at next meeting of the Board".

While the Directors deliberated over the larger picture, in the background negotiations and work continued. The Engineering and Estates Committee, on 27th April 1898, had to discuss the Public Library in Lower Marsh, Lambeth. A letter of 20th April from the Solicitor pointed out the library was scheduled in the Company's bill, and that the Lambeth Vestry required that before it was interfered with the L&SWR should, at their own expense, erect another library and librarian's residence on a new site, also paying £500 to the Vestry for removal and related costs. This was not to be the last or only example of people seeking a high price from the L&SWR for expansion needs now beyond any land the L&SWR had originally owned.

In the background others, not within the L&SWR, continued to have their concerns - the 11th May 1898 Engineering and Estates meeting, for example, discussing Nobles and Hoare's premises. Nobles and Hoare were a well-established company of colour and varnish makers and dealers who ironically had moved into railway varnishes, and manufactured near Waterloo Junction but had other premises near Waterloo Station on Holmes Terrace. One of the partners in Nobles and Hoare was Joseph Rolls Hoare who was also a Director of the London Tilbury and Southend Railway of which he became Deputy Chairman in 1911. The L&SWR Solicitor reported and was duly instructed having explained the proposed terms for meeting the

Lady Diana Cooper divided her time between London and Paris, using the Boat Trains out of Waterloo.

objections of Nobles and Hoare. The Committee also discussed the public Library and the terms required by the Lambeth Vestry and London County Council (LCC) for properties in Lower Marsh.

Meanwhile, on 11th July 1898, the fiftieth anniversary of the opening of the Waterloo Bridge station, The Drain was opened by the Duke of Cambridge, (the public opening was on 8th August delayed because of a fire in the arches close to the line). The Waterloo and City was absorbed into the L&SWR, under the provisions of an L&SWR Act of 20th July 1906, on 1st January 1907 testament to consistency of vision of reaching the City. "The Drain" was the only tube-line, after the creation of the London Passenger Transport Board on 1st July 1933, to remain independent being operated by successive mainline railway companies until 1994 when transferred to London Underground.

Clearly matters were not progressing satisfactorily and agreement was not being reached so, as is the recognised practice in these matters, at the 13th October 1898 Court of Directors a special committee was appointed consisting of the Chairman, Deputy Chairman, Mr Scott and the members of the Engineering and Estates Committee. The Special Committee had powers to look at all matters "to report from time to time to the Board" and meet when required by the Chairman or in his absence his Deputy".

The Special Committee met speedily on 25th October 1898 and decided on properties delineated within an area to north and south of "station and east side of Waterloo Road and with addition of the houses adjoining, on the east, the site in Narrow Wall but omitting the Chapel and Baths sites in the York Road"

That communications be opened by the General Manager, Solicitor and engineer, with the London County Council, Lambeth Vestry, & All Saints Church & School Authorities in explanation of the Company's plans with a view to making the necessary arrangements" . Although a far cry from the 1848 era of almost unilateral action these decisions were ratified by the 27th October 1898 Court of Directors meeting.

Following the 5th January 1899 meeting of the Court of Directors which discussed the progress of the Bill, the 2nd February Court of Directors was advised the Bill had passed Standing Orders unopposed and awaited introduction into Parliament and the decision was taken to seek a meeting with the LCC about the subject of the station enlargement. The L&SWR's solicitor and engineer met the Chairman of the LCC Parliamentary Committee following which the 15th February 1899 Special Committee were told the LCC were offering a meeting with their Parliamentary committee at 4-30 on Thursday 23rd February , an offer they accepted.

The 16th February 1899 Court of Directors meeting ratified the Special Committee decision, the delegation to be Chairman, Deputy, Mr Portal and Mr Scott. The meeting also instructed the solicitor to arrange the date for unification of All Saints and St John's Parishes; to decline the terms proposed by the Cannon Brewery Company for the purchase of their leasehold interest in premises at Granby Place, and Aubin Street; and instructed in the matter of Messrs Nobles and Hoare. Because Waterloo Station's location affected the affairs of three other railways: the SER, "The Drain", and Necropolis the L&SWR Directors also Agreed to "matters requiring adjustment with them [Waterloo and City] in connection with the Powers over their property at Waterloo included in this Company's Bill for the ensuing Session of Parliament" and the terms of the new arrangement with the Necropolis Company were explained to the Board by the solicitor. Essentially the Necropolis Company exploited their powerful position insisting on new stock for their train, a perpetual rent-free lease on new premises, free transit of goods for use in the cemetery. The Necropolis Company also obtained powers to decide the details of the new station that was to be provided by the L&SWR, £32,000 compensation for the loss of the old station, transfer of the HQ and there was to be no limit to the number of mourners using the service who could now return not just by any train to Waterloo but also Clapham Junction or Vauxhall. It would cost the L&SWR £5,500 to purchase land for the new station, and a further £43,494 to build the station (the LNNMC paying a further £1,500 for "extras" not agreed at the time of specification). Necropolis may not have traded to the original commercial expectations, but they were not a dead loss when it came to exploiting their position – a position ironically strengthened by earlier negotiations with the L&SWR.

Tacitly recognising the complexities of the modern age, so much greater than when the station was originally built and railways had such hegemony the 27th April 1899 Court of Directors instructed the solicitor to "continue negotiations with the London County Council and the other petitioners against the Bill". The Court also instructed that Lambeth Vestry were to be written to inviting them to send a deputation to meet the Directors; and that the "Chairman and other Directors" had met the North Lambeth Re-Housing Committee on 18th April.

That the Necropolis Company had withdrawn their petition was reported to the 8th June 1899 Court of Directors meeting. The solicitor reported at the Director's meeting, on 22nd June 1899, the Bill had passed through the Committee of the Lords. However the solicitor, "explained the provision inserted therein at the instance of

Messrs Nobles & Hoare to the effect that if their property is required the Company are to give them Notice to Treat within 3 months after the passing of the Act".

By the 2nd August 1899 Engineering and Estates meeting the solicitor was able to highlight that: On 1st November 1899, in an amazing irony itself the date of All Saints, the church of All Saints would cease to be a separate parish. However the Church of England insisted the railway had to find a new site and pay £4,500 "for a new edifice" with possession of the existing site not to be taken until 12 months after conveyance of new site. All Saints school had to be found a site and £4,000 paid for the erection of a new school, with possession of the existing site not gained until nine months after conveyance of the new site. The "retiring" incumbent of All Saints was, from 1st November, to receive from the Company £350 p.a. or the difference if he accepted preferment. The Necropolis Railway found their resistance to the Bill overcome by an agreement that the L&SWR would erect new buildings on which they would also grant a 999 year lease with a nominal rent, and pay £6,000 on taking possession of old premises and £6,000 within 28 days of reinstatement in new premises. The Necropolis Company did however agree the L&SWR could remove the stop block and use the line at Waterloo on receipt of Royal Assent. The LCC concerns secured agreement that, on or before 31st December 1899, the Company was to invest £30,000 for future road schemes, in names of two Trustees, the dividends of which were to accumulate at compound interest; the L&SWR was to provide a thoroughfare for pedestrians not less than 12' wide in line of York Street (now Leake Street). The LCC also secured agreement the railway would provide details of the scheme for "labouring class" dwellings in Boniface Street and would not interfere with the Fire Brigade Station, at the corner of Waterloo Road and Holmes Terrace until a new site was found. (The Fire station was ultimately located further down Waterloo Road, opened on 23rd June 1910 by the Chairman of the Fire Brigade Committee of the LCC, the plaque recording no mention of the L&SWR's contribution. It is now a rather agreeable wine bar.) In return the LCC did not oppose any application to widen the Railway over Westminster Bridge Road or close York Street to vehicular traffic, or the closure of Robert Street, portions of Mepham Street, Frances Street and Agnes Street. Finally, that with regard to Nobles and Hoare any Notice to Treat was to be served within three months meaning by 19th August 1899.

Accordingly the L&SWR's solicitor was able to confirm to the Court of Directors on 3rd August 1899 that the Bill was no longer contentious and it duly received Royal Assent.

New century new station

Despite the planning of a new station the daily operation still had to go on, hardly surprising given that Waterloo Station had entered the new Century in 1900 with some 50,000 passengers using around 800 trains a day in winter. In summer the figures for Waterloo use were nearer a daily average of 80,000 in 1,040 trains and Waterloo was struggling to cope. So it was that in 1901 the North Station became the first part of the Waterloo ensemble to embrace the idea of the closed off platform. In the following month, on 20th February, Rohans began their long association with Waterloo Station when they opened a flower and fruit stall for an annual rental of £75.

It was still not wholly clear, Parliamentary approval notwithstanding, what the L&SWR were planning. The 11th April 1900 meeting of the Court of Directors deferred consideration until they met at 1.45 on 26th April 1900. The reconvened Court of Directors decided that the Engineering and Estates Committee was authorised to make the additions to the south side of the Station "subject to the necessary consent being first obtained from the London County Council and the Lambeth Vestry to the proposed deviation of the new road into the Lower Marsh"

The Engineering and Estates meeting of 23rd May 1900, faced with a Report from the Engineer with plans and estimates for new roofing over Platforms 1 to 4 and part of the cab yard proposing three options:

- in type similar to existing roof £13,750,

• as part of ultimate Scheme for station enlargement and at a higher level £17,500,

• Repairs necessary to secure stability of existing roof £350,

recommended the £17,500 scheme to the Board, which recommendation was accepted.

Overall the Company had to proceed cautiously because profits were variable and there were other demands on the Company's finances. It was also true that the rates of returns on the railways were diminishing even at this era, largely as costs rose with increased labour rates and other demands to be met. This caution did not stop the addition of another "Nock-ian" "gargoyle" from the Central Station! In October 1900 approval was given for a structure over the cab road approach to North Station/Main Line arrivals at Central Station which would be punched through the wall of Central Station at platform level, but this time running parallel to Waterloo Road. The new excrescence was a wooden structure, perhaps recognising that a new station was imminent, and was to relocate season-ticket staff from the stygian office in an arch under the station.

The LNER Mallard arriving in Waterloo during the 1948 Exchange Trials to find the best locomotive designs.

Nevertheless it did not add to the classical harmony of the original building – although having been already defiled it may be suggested it did not ruin it either!

To begin the new station works was going to be more difficult than previous builds because there was no longer a plethora of "green field" space which the railway could build on – land clearance was needed. The Necropolis Station was relocated swiftly, commensurate with works to relocate local residents, and the new Necropolis Station, completed by 8th February, being opened on 16th February 1902.

With some land cleared the Engineering and Estates Committee were thus able to consider and approve, on 30th April 1902, giving approval to widen Platform 3 because of increasing passenger demand. For £520, a timber extension would widen the platform to an appreciable length of the former No. 6 platform road, whereupon No. 5 road which had hitherto served the connection to the SER, would be realigned to serve the newly widened platform. The Committee also received detailed plans from the Engineer for enlargement on the "south" side. The Engineer sought authority for quantities and invite tenders for "the foundation work and arches to up to platform surface level [the cost of which he estimated at £222,000] leaving the roofing and buildings to be dealt with hereafter under a separate contract" which was approved.

The next Engineering and Estates meeting of 22 July 1902 , whilst also recognising that the approach at Westminster Bridge Road was an area needing attention found that detailed drawings and approximate quantities for the authorised foundation works were advanced enough to let the contract, so the letter offering a list of firms to approach was agreed and authorised. Even while the new station was underway, increasing traffic meant the L&SWR had to fund more approach tracks and they therefore considered widening their bridge over Westminster Bridge Road. The glamour of a station is always dependent on the approach rails which generally form a pinch-point and the L&SWR had come a long way from thinking four was enough. However just as an ocean-liner was pretty useless without tugs, so splendid new stations were no use if they had no suitable access lines! Because of the extra work performed in the schedule of prices the Engineer also asked for a bonus of £20 for Mr Hawes and this was also agreed.

Mr Hawes was not the only one feeling things were coming up roses at Waterloo. In July 1902 Rohans had the same faith in the long-term future of Waterloo as the Court of Directors, and extended their flower-stall operations to the South Station.

Setting the seeds for growth in 1903 enabled site clearance and the letting of contracts for sub-structure work. Indeed, at this time, there was little sign of actual building because works were about sub-structures, realigning approach roads, strengthening existing arches, and combating the marshy ground inherent in an area called Lower Marsh Road! In fact not only was the land marshy, which given English stolidity in naming places might have been expected from the name of the road, but one of London's lost rivers was discovered, although it was not clear whether it was the Lock Stream or the Effra Delta. Other early, and less obvious, works making erecting the station possible included the building of a new and modern Church school in Exton Street, and the artisans' dwelling blocks. Five of the artisan's blocks were built on the site of Maudslay's former engineering works, the former southern half of Pedlar's Acre at the rear of the current Bakerloo station, which had been let to Maudsley Sons and Field since 1810 but the land had reverted to the Lambeth Borough Council in 1900; and one block at Stangate.

Clearance of the land and properties started immediately and was pivotal since it gave new ground to the Company which would thereby allow three new tracks to be built on operationally virgin land next to the existing No. 1 line of South Station (roughly where the current No 4 platform now is). Building the three lines would make possible the demolition of the old South Station and several station offices between the Central and South Stations. Through needing to demolish the offices it was imperative therefore that a start be made on the new office block, which would separate the cab rank and the concourse, in its current location.

The design of the main approach from the Westminster Bridge Road, raised at the meeting of 23rd July 1902, was discussed again at the 21st January 1903 meeting of the Engineering and Estates Committee. The Engineer's design showing intent to construct the road approach to Waterloo under the railway supported by columns in the centre of the roadway and was duly approved. The 18th March meeting saw, further consideration of models for the new station and a decision to refer to the Board the request from the engineer that it was necessary to provide new office accommodation for the staff of the Traffic, Goods and Audit Department which offices he considered might be provided on a site fronting the York Road.

Away from plans and concepts Waterloo suffered one of its thankfully infrequent accidents on the 5th May 1904. An empty milk-train set off and collided with a passenger train killing one passenger. The subsequent inquiry established that a signal linesman undertaking repairs had accidentally stepped on a signal wire which had moved the signal to the "clear" position.

The constraints on the land site under L&SWR ownership were such that at the 8th February 1905 Engineering and Estates meeting the solicitor shewed a map with all the properties they owned, and those they had an interest in, and those they had approval by Parliament to buy, which approvals expire "August next", meaning it was felt the Company needed more land The meeting also authorised the widening of the bridge over Westminster Bridge Road, considered the engineer's recommendation about buying steel and ironwork to construct part of the highway needed from Lower Marsh and, imaginatively, to be named Spur Road. Proposals were tabled to purchase the iron and steel from the Horseley Company on same terms and prices as at Waterloo, which had been accepted by the Engineering and Estates Committee on 25th January, thereby leading to approval at 3rd May 1905 Engineering and Estates Committee.

The acquisition of more properties in Westminster Bridge Road was hampered when, at the 28th June 1905 Engineering and Estates meeting, a letter from the estate agent of 9th June was read. The estate agent stated that Wilkinson's Trustees asked £37,500 for their interest less a fair allowance in respect of the leasehold portion, which was estimated by the estate agent at £3,500, but they would consider an offer by the Company. This offer was duly reported to the Board with a recommendation from the Committee that the General Manager, Secretary, and Engineer report further on the question of office accommodation.

At this point the actual works underway at the station were less of a problem than acquiring land. The engineer wrote on 26th June that Messrs Perry were now completing the portion of work authorised by the Minute of 30th April 1902 and recommended a schedule of prices be placed with them, "for the work above rail level, excluding the steelwork to screen wall and roof, the cost of which he estimated at £40,000. This estimate does not include any new Station offices, or covering over the new circulating area or cab-yard, the whole of which will form the subject of an additional contract". The Engineering and Estates Committee approved the Engineer's recommendation which was then ratified by the 29th June 1905 meeting of the Court of Directors.

On 13th July 1905 the Court of Directors received the deliberations of their various department heads and ordered that "the purchase of Atkinson's premise in the Westminster Bridge Road be not entertained." The rampant days of railway expansion were clearly over, ransoms could be paid and indeed would be, but capital was no longer so abundant that "King Railway" could or would acquire everything.

More successfully, and more operationally imperative, the L&SWR Engineer was able to report to the 4th October 1905 Engineering and Estates Committee that the designs for the bridge over Westminster Bridge Road were approved by both councils. The designs included, "the provision of a notice board relating to the company's business on the face of the bridge" and whereupon it was agreed that detailed drawings would be brought up.

If rail access to Waterloo had to be improved by bridges, road access was to be improved by a tunnel. Road improvements included the new approach from Westminster Bridge Road which curved from the entrance gates on the station's north side by a tunnel under the full width of the railway and which connected with the Lower Marsh at the other end and was a very wide wood-paved structure, with a pavement itself some 12' wide, but at 1:25 gradient . Much work continued to be done at weekends since it necessitated demolition of many of the original arches, replacing them with girder bridges, to support the railway tracks above.

In November 1905 the new station works became more obvious when works commenced on the new roof and steelwork began to be erected over the existing roof of South Station. The roof was a major achievement, as station roofs often were and would continue to be, being supported by octagonal built up steel columns from platform to roof, roughly 60' apart, and these columns themselves stood on brick piers which went down to the foundations. The roof was ridged at right angles to the track until reaching the concourse when it became perpendicular to that. Carried on 12" deep girders the roof was secured at one end into the south wall which itself was surmounted by a cast-iron glazed screen designed to increase lighting and at the other end of the roof was a screen which reached some 20' above the rail-lines.

The detailed plans for the bridge at Westminster Bridge Road, having been agreed by the municipal authorities the Engineer stating that, to rail level, the approximate cost of the works was £17,000 so he sought and obtained approval on 21st February 1906 to go out to tender. The tender from the Cleveland Bridge Engineering Co for this supply and fixing of the steel and wrought iron work at £4,787. 10.11 was accepted at the 4th April 1906 Engineering and Estates meeting.

The Baker Street and Waterloo Railway (very speedily dubbed by the public the Bakerloo which name has stayed with us officially) ran from Baker Street under the West End to the Elephant and Castle had had financial problems, and was another tube line not assisted by the L&SWR, but it finally reached Waterloo in 1906. Located on the street level, below the northern edge of the L&SWR terminal, the

Queen Victoria famously disliked rail travel, but relented when the LSWR built a special station for her at Windsor.

tube station, placed between those of Embankment and Lambeth North was opened on 10th March. The line itself went in a sharp curve swinging round from beneath the river to head on towards what is now Lambeth North, was at the time Kennington Road, and in July 1906 would become renamed Westminster Bridge Road before becoming Lambeth North in April 1917. Stairs and a slope to the North Station concourse served those changing from tube station to mainline station. Access to the Tube was via a lift from the rather small Bakerloo Line booking office, adjacent to York Road, and located at the western end of the subway that ran under the L&SWR's Waterloo.

On the 18th April 1906 Mr Macaulay had authorised the acceptance of the tender from Messrs Eastwood Swingler & Co for the supply and fixing of iron and steel to complete the spur approach to the station from Lower Marsh. The tender was for £4,371/17/2 and had been recommended to Macaulay by the Engineer. This decision was approved 2nd May 1906 Engineering and Estates Committee.

Not all was major structural works however. Communications were to be improved after a proposal of 7th May 1906 from the L&SWR to accept the terms of a Contract with Samson Pneumatic Tube Company at 20 Cheapside London to the value of £362/10/0. Signed on 2nd July 1906 "…to build and install at their Waterloo Station a system of Pneumatic Dispatch tubes at the price of three hundred and sixty two pounds ten shillings" the works to be completed by 5TH September 1906. The system was Samson's "Standard" which gave a continuous service at will. Primarily intended for communication between the Telegraph Office and the Traffic Superintendent's Office there was to be sufficient power from the True Circle Blower, driven by an electric motor, to give additional connections between the offices on the North Station and the Telegraph Office. These tubes allowed the seamlessly drawn brass carrier tubes on 2 ¼" O.D. and 20 S.W.G. (Outside Diameter and Standard Wire Gauge) to be conveyed along a system with the exposed tubing being made of "bright polished brass". However the use of such technology did not and would not preclude the use of telephones to also improve office efficiency.

The L&SWR at Waterloo Station may have been landlocked, and was often held to ransom by various agencies and the SER would in the near future, but those that thought the Company would buy anything were sometimes frustrated. At the 27th June 1906 Engineering and Estates meeting an Estate Agent's letter of 22nd June was reported with a communication from Messrs Lumleys offering Atkinson's Premises again to the Company for the reduced sum of £27,000. This was merely referred to the Board who declined the offer the following day.

Between 1906 and 1908, to allow for 11 tracks on the immediate approach to the station, works on the bridge over Westminster Bridge Road were undertaken. This necessitated building a lattice of girders spanning 90' and of a 12' depth on the outside with arched rib girders on the inside - at all times having to make sure double-decker trams could pass.

Works were considered so satisfactory at the new South Station that the Engineer's letter of 26th July, to 1st August 1906 Engineering and Estates Committee, saying Messrs Perry & Co would like a release of some of the retention fees for their work in widening the South Side was favourably considered. From the retained sum of £12,895 the Engineer recommended £6,000 be released and this the Board agreed to.

Growing traffic meant, on 22nd May 1907, the Company requested permission for works between Waterloo and Clapham Junction were approved by the Board of Trade on 25th May subject to "inspection when complete." On 28th May 1908 the L&SWR wrote again to the Board of Trade to, "shew the alterations between Waterloo Station and the B box". However, against the background of increasing traffic, was also the beginning of signs that the car would impact at the top end of the passengers. The L&SWR had always, for example, had a lucrative trade to Ascot but at Royal Hunt Cup day in 1907 1,116 motor cars were spotted at the race course.

Meanwhile, at the A box, McKenzie & Holland Limited, of the Vulcan Iron works Worcester, tendered on 26th August 1907 for electrical interlocking and block work at a price of £1,650. The Tender was accepted on 10th October 1907 however the WR Sykes Interlocking Signal Company Limited claimed that using McKenzie & Holland was an infringement of their Patent Rights. Accordingly McKenzie and Holland supplied an indemnity, on 25th June 1908, "against all actions, accounts, claims and demands by the Sykes Company or any other person or persons whomsoever for or in respect of the infringement or alleged infringement..."

The international trade that Waterloo attracted, thanks in the main to their boat links, was affirmed when, in November 1908, the

An early morning photo taken in 1914 shows the suburban electrics ready to start their day's work.

Company made formal arrangements for the acceptance of Traveller's Cheques. On 5th November, the L&SWR's Traffic Committee gave authority to safeguard Traveller's Cheques and agreed on the 25th to take the United States Express Company Traveller's Cheques at Waterloo, Southampton and Plymouth stations subject to indemnification against loss damages and costs through forgery or theft. The indemnity was forthcoming on 27th November.

The initial phase of the new station contained five Ferro-concrete platforms. The first two platforms, and three roads, of the new station came into use on 24th June 1909, which even though these particular works were on additional land signalled the end of South Station because it could now be demolished. Platform 4 speedily followed into service, on 25th July 1909, and this platform was, approximately, where the first platform of the former South Station had been. The new platform replacements were much straighter than the originals, which were often fan shaped, and were built in concrete with Ferro-concrete tops tastefully set off by slate copings quarried from

Delabole in Cornwall. Within and under the platforms were the usual cables and pipes inherent on the running of a railway. New platforms were often connected by stairs on a long passageway to the York Road. This passageway connected to the platforms for "The Drain" as well as the booking office for the Bakerloo Line. Those wishing to leave "The Drain" for Waterloo Road were catered for via other passageways, which also gave access to the concourse.

It was along the passageway leading to the Waterloo Road that there were a variety of doors which were not always clearly understood or perhaps even noticed by various travellers - they certainly mystified me. Over the years behind those doors were located variously staff canteens, clubs for staff, rifle ranges, police offices and lost property. Both these passages were also put to other uses at various times - the one to York Road had part of it used as a free buffet for servicemen between December 1915 and April 1920 a plaque recording that over 8 million soldiers and sailors (the poor Air Force seemingly left to starve!) had free meals there. Perhaps somewhat less gallantly the other passage, to Waterloo Road, contained at some periods accommodation for emigrants who the L&SWR did not want mingling with regular passengers in their new waiting rooms.

1909 also saw a start made, at the south-eastern corner, on building new offices and public facilities behind the new concourse whilst Platform 5 came into service on 6th March 1910. It is, incidentally, from this time that the L&SWR embraced the far from innovative concept of numbering all platform faces.

When the original South Station was built passengers had been somewhat inconvenienced by the decision to place a locomotive yard part-between South and Central Stations However, when new platforms similar to those on the former South Station were erected, that decision was revisited. An enlarged yard of the South Sidings near Necropolis, the station for those facing their final rest, became the yard for "at rest" locomotives. The Windsor Line yards and turntable were ultimately also to be relocated nearer York Road at the other end of the station.

Passenger flows being more like a logjam than a swirling tide of humanity at Waterloo hitherto it was probably with some relief that the L&SWR could address the connection to the SER. The SER had an operational accommodation with the London Chatham and Dover Railway and usage of the through connection had significantly decreased. On 11th October 1910, W.F. Marwood of the Board of Trade wrote a memo that Sir Charles Owens, the General Manager of the L&SWR, and Mr Bishop, solicitor to the Company, had seen Major Pringle and himself on the topic of the connecting railway line. The L&SWR now reviewed their enthusiasm for the link to the Charing Cross- London Bridge line and took the view there was no obligation to maintain the connecting line in the 1859 Act, pointed out that no trains had run into Cannon Street over the line for many years past, and it was only being used for milk traffic, seven milk vans being dealt with daily. The L&SWR delegation advised the erection of fresh offices at the end of their terminus, must perforce cross the existing junction line, and the proposed cab yard would also extend from one side of the station to the other thereby also crossing the present line of rails. Owens promised provision for foot passengers commuting between the two stations, and to make a deal with their railway neighbours about milk traffic, if the line was closed.

The Board of Trade party pointed out concerns "...that the connecting line might possibly at some time be of great importance in the movement of troops". They insisted that Sir Charles, himself a Lieutenant Colonel, should discuss this matter with the War Office even though Sir Charles had pointed out there were connections between the L&SWR/SER at Clapham Junction and Guildford. The following day, in the interim between the meeting with the L&SWR and War Office the memo was annotated:-

"The abandonment of the existing connection between Waterloo Station and Waterloo Junction station (SE&C Ry) will not minimize the present public facilities, and on general public grounds I think we cannot object to the proposal.

If for special military purposes the connection is held to be necessary, it would be possible I think to preserve it, without materially affecting the company's building scheme, except perhaps aesthetically"

The meeting between the L&SWR and the War Office duly took place, the War Office writing to Sir Charles Owens on 1st November 1910. E.W. Ward wrote "The Army Council have considered the question which you discussed with the Quartermaster General and myself about a fortnight ago.......and I am glad to be able to tell you that they have no objection to the proposal"

To appease the LCC Parliamentary Committee the L&SWR agreed to provide a "suitable and sufficient means of communication" for pedestrians between the two main-line railway stations, indeed the Board of Trade had sought clarification on this point, after the meeting with Sir Charles, their recollection being unclear. Owens confirmed on 16th November 1910, "....It is quite true that provision has been made in the scheme for the convenience of foot passengers between our Station and the South Eastern and Chatham Company's Station and the footway across the new cab yard will be under cover and on the level." Marwood therefore confirmed, on 22nd November, that because the War Office had no objection to moving the connecting line through Waterloo Station nor would the Board of Trade.

Meanwhile, on tracks the railways did want to run trains on, timekeeping was still an issue. The railways had played an enormous role in imposing "standard time" across the country to suit the exigencies of a consistent timetable. Standard time was almost universal in England by 1852 (save for Cornwall still not connected to the main railway system) and edging throughout the rest of the island also, although it was not to be a matter of legislative reality until 1880, but having done that through the timetable it was imperative that the clocks all kept to a standard time - especially on and within each station. So at Waterloo, in 1910, time-keeping switched to the new "Synchronome" system. The Synchronome system relied on one electrically-driven pendulum master clock which could operate any number of clock faces all of which lacked any clock-work in the accepted sense and instead had a single wheel to the rear which also meant they occupied less space and could be easily illuminated. Additionally, in line with the L&SWR's attempts to be a railway for the new century, there were considerable cost savings in the new streamlined time-keeping system. Sixty dials were fitted at Waterloo in 1910, the master clock (and its back-up) synchronised daily with Greenwich via the Post Office, powering clocks within the offices and on the platforms. There were to be five more extensions of the Synchronome system over the years leading to the opening of the new station with its 240 clocks varying from the ordinary dial in the offices at 12" to the big four-faced turret clock with its 6' faces.

Clocks sorted, and the lack of Civil Service resistance, encouraged the L&SWR to believe it was timely to include application for the abandoning of the line in the L&SWR Bill which was duly tabled 1 and 2 Geo V – Session 1911. The Bill was "...to empower the London and South Western Railway Company to construct new street and other works and to acquire additional lands to authorise the abandonment of existing works of the Company and the South Eastern Railway Company; to confer further powers on the Company and other companies in respect of superfluous lands to provide for the transfer to the Company and for other purposes (South Western Railway). The single-track link however, by agreement, had gone out of use on 26th March 1911,

In Parliament matters were proceeding smoothly. The Bill had been read for the first time on 17th May 1911 and for the second time on 29th May. However to ensure no obstacles it was still necessary to appease the SER. If the L&SWR had been in the driving seat when it came to leaning on the SER to allow the connecting spur in the middle of the previous century the latter company seemed to exact a high price when the L&SWR wanted to reverse that policy. Heads of Agreement between the L&SWR, SEC Railway's Management Committee and the SER on 20th May 1911 showed a cartel of geographic spheres of influence and sorted out arrangements for Aldershot which was to the SER's benefit. To acquire certain lands the L&SWR needed for the new station meant buying land from the SER (who also owned the Hole in the Wall pub!)

who extracted very good terms in exchange for which the SER agreed not to oppose the L&SWR's Bill in Parliament's pending session. The L&SWR also got the line closure they wanted:-

The South Western Company shall be at liberty if and when the said Bill shall become law to abandon and discontinue the use of the Junction of their Railway with the Branch Railway at the north east end of Waterloo Station and on the discontinuation of the use of the

An unexploded bomb goes on show at Waterloo under the watchful eyes of the Home Guard in 1940.

said Junction the South Western Company shall provide a properly paved foot-crossing under cover upon which vehicles shall not be permitted to stand between such Station and the Waterloo Junction Station of the Managing Committee. The South Western Company shall also cause all milk traffic (including empty cans) consigned via Waterloo to or from any Station on the Railway of the Managing Committee and coming from or to the Railway of the South Western Company to be transferred to and from the Railway of the Managing Committee at such a point on the existing Bridge over Waterloo Road as the respective Superintendents of the Lines of Railway of the South Western Company and the Managing Committee shall from time to time agree."

The L&SWR was also to pay the costs of making good the remaining SER track from the junction, maintain part of a bridge over Waterloo Road, and pay for the arches of the Managing Committee and other works as a consequence of the alteration to any road levels in Frances Street, Agnes Street and Mepham Street. In the event of dispute arbitration was to be by the Board of Trade.

Meanwhile, perhaps more happily, works at Waterloo were progressed such that the opening of the spacious Booking Hall, on 11th June 1911, was possible. This was also the year, 1911, that Sir Hugh Henry John William Drummond became Chairman of the L&SWR, having been appointed Deputy in 1903 after joining the Board in 1900, and started a slightly more focussed and dynamic regime.

In the rarefied air of Westminster and the powerful figures there the Company's Bill received a Report from Committee with amendments on 15th June 1911. The amendments, and existence of the Bill, provided a behind the scenes threat to delay its Parliamentary progress. The L&SWR's handling of special trains, usually run from Waterloo, was not always well appreciated. At the time of the Spithead/Coronation review, 24th June 1911, questions were asked in the House about the fact that some MPs had been charged for a First-Class ticket and not received a First-Class seat. In reply Mr McKenna pointed out the Admiralty had invited 6,500 guests and the railway company had said at the beginning of the contract that they could not guarantee that number of seats were available of that class. At the time ordinary First-Class return fare from Waterloo to Southampton was 23/- reduced to 16/6 at the weekend. The Admiralty Board had negotiated a price of £1 a seat but some MPs were still affronted not to have travelled First-Class.

In fact the L&SWR only had 183 purely First-Class carriages, which included old six-wheelers unsuited to high-speed running, and had for some years been building composite carriages. The Company pointed out that the Admiralty's guests had used 17 special trains and London alone had supplied another 19. Despite a number of threatened Parliamentary obstructions from those MPs irate about their travel arrangements (does much change?) the L&SWR Bill of 1911 consideration of amendments was tolerably uncontroversial and the Bill received a Third Reading, on 18th July, which was passed subject to a few amendments.

On 21st July the Lords agreed to the Commons' amendments and the Bill received Royal Assent on 18th August 1911. The L&SWR, whatever the price and it was a high one, had secured the Bill's passage by averting opposition. No Committee evidence was taken for the London and South Western Railway Bill and there is no record of Opposed Private Bill evidence taken for the Bill in the Commons. In the Lords, the Bill is noted in an Opposed Private Bill Committee volume as only stating that 'no evidence was taken'.

By 18th December 1911 travelling passengers were rewarded with the new vehicle roadway, from Westminster Bridge Road, revealing the new Booking Hall. The L&SWR having at the start of the new works built inclined roadways from both Lower Marsh and Westminster Bridge Road, and now connecting those two points to serve all the station seemed a potent symbol they were embracing the idea of the "whole station" experience.

In 1912 Herbert A. Walker became General Manager of the L&SWR and the pairing with Hugh Drummond brought a new impetus to proceedings, arguably the first sign of which was the Board authorising progress to go through in steady planned stages.

Harry Hopkins, adviser to US President Roosevelt leaves London in January 1941 after meeting Churchill.

At a meeting of the L&SWR Board of 26th July 1912 it was decided that works were indeed to be done in the order decided by the Chief Engineer but with the important proviso that they were to be done in consultation with the General Manager. The era of laissez faire planning for passengers at Waterloo was now arguably as dead as those conveyed by the LNMMC. Having had three years to recover from the radicalism of numbering platform faces it was also in October 1912 that the L&SWR ended laissez faire platform numbering, Jackson dating 1st October as the day platforms were renumbered in sequence. Any confusion now was likely to be of briefer duration since the L&SWR would now number platforms consecutively, but the erection of new platforms would mean some would have a number for a short period before being "christened" with a new number again.

Despite the total L&SWR paid up capital (including Loans and Debenture Stock) being £56,000,000 at the year end of 1912, with signs of a decline in suburban traffic from the inner suburbs, Walker considered fewer than 23 platforms would be needed thereby removing the need to expand the station any further to the west meaning considerable financial savings would also be made by keeping the still structurally sound roof of the 1885 Windsor Station. The wisdom of the decision to reduce the number of platforms was to be reinforced when, by the end of 1912, the L&SWR had electric trains, with their quicker turnaround times, on their planning horizon.

The inconvenient offices along Platform 1 were largely gone by 1913 and, reflecting improvements on the arrival to the station, new wider stairways had been built linking the concourse to the Waterloo and City Line as well as Waterloo Road. Walker applied to the Board of Trade, 22nd April 1913, about new works to the station, the plans shewing the new roof over the South Station, and sanction was granted on 1st May 1913, "whole of the" being manually inserted between "approved" and "the works" on the standard form. The Board of Trade commented on there being no details sent regarding signalling works to which the Company replied to, inter alia, "The plans of the proposed new signalling arrangements are not yet definitely settled, but they shall be submitted to the Department in due course."

Following a fact-finding mission to the Liverpool - Southport line of Lancashire & Yorkshire Railway, who had been using a DC conductor rail collector system since 1904, the L&SWR publicly announced they were to electrify their innermost suburban lines from Waterloo in 1913.

The buildings of the new station had progressed far enough that the Surrey Room, along with the slightly less salubrious circular buffet on the concourse, were opened on 27th June 1913 – hardly surprisingly marked by a lunch laid on for Directors and guests.

Dining was however an ancillary function of the railway, although no doubt the gentlemen using Spartan Waterloo Bridge in 1848 would have probably even been grateful for the later curled BR sandwich. Two days after the opening of the Surrey Room the new Platform 6 was opened platform development now well and truly in areas where trains had always been. However there could be no question of wholesale retention of existing platforms since older platforms needed reconstructing in concrete, with lengthening and realignment, to accommodate the new electric trains which were due for introduction in 1915.

Remorselessly works progressed in a steady advance: in July 1913, the Crows Nest Signal box was removed, and by the end of the year, on 7th December, there was a new Platform 11 thereby causing the existing Platforms 9 to 17 to be renumbered Platforms 12 to 20. However having removed the historic railway line crossing a concourse a 50' wide central cab road was provided across the new concourse ,between Platforms 11 and 12, serviced at one end, via a tunnel, from Griffin Street and at the other through a central archway in the office block opposite Platforms 11 and 12. To either side of the archway were generous oblong pedestrian openings and above the arch ensemble, the Company's office block right to the end of the Windsor Line concourse was projected, these offices being built above the suburban booking office, waiting rooms and yet more refreshment facilities. The office block would also serve to separate the concourse from the new vehicle highway. L&SWR train movements were augmented the following year with the creation of a new locomotive yard on 1st March 1914 and the opening of a new Platform 19 on 14th June.

However the Kaiser had movement plans of his own and triggered off The Great War by invading "Gallant Little Belgium", the modern State wherein Wellington had defeated the Corsican Upstart at the Battle that named the bridge from which the station took its name. In war-time office buildings were not seen as a priority but Waterloo, serving the south coast, was important for British troop movements. Ironically only a month before, on 18th July 1914, the L&SWR had been running 30/- (including luncheon and tea as well as boat conveyance) "Special First Class Return" trips to Spithead to see the King inspect the fleet at a "Record array of Warships".

War did not totally stop modernisation of Waterloo Station with a new Platform 20 opening on 14th February 1915 swiftly followed a fortnight later by a new Platform 21. A new Platform 17 and 18 on 11th April preceded a new Platform 16 on 13th June 1915 as Waterloo adjusted to war movements.

With the rush to modernity and arrival of new platforms the L&SWR did not forget its heritage making sure an old carriage arrived in homage to their roots. Railway companies were given to laying claim to an earlier pedigree than they actually had, such claims often resting on the fact they had bought or absorbed an earlier railway company or line. The L&SWR was no exception and liked to date itself from 1832 because it contained the Bodmin & Wadebridge Railway (opened 4th July 1834, but sanctioned by Parliament, in 1832, and acquired by the L&SWR in 1845 for £35,000 although it would not actually be connected to the L&SWR until 1895). For this reason the L&SWR displayed an example of the Bodmin & Wadebridge four-wheeled closed composite First and Second Class Carriage on a plinth on the new concourse from 26th July 1915. Located opposite Platform 9 this relic of the 1830s had been refurbished at the Eastleigh works and stood on granite sleepers – part of the original permanent way.

If Waterloo Station was adjusting to war-time demands and accommodating new platforms or old carriages it was also rolling out the new power. The Waterloo to Wimbledon via East Putney service was the first service electrified on 25th October 1915 which made operational sense given the decision to store electric units there rather than at congested Waterloo. Electric roll-out continued: Twickenham, Kingston, and Shepperton services (from Clapham Junction) 30th January 1916, Hounslow loop 12th March 1916, and Hampton Court on 18th June. The electricity for the suburban services was not coming from Waterloo but Durnsford Road at Wimbledon; a source opened in 1915 during one war, bombed by the Germans in the next and, despite that, the power-station lasted until 1958. On the main-line, Platforms 1 to 6 also commenced electrification from 30th January 1916.

In the following month the L&SWR entered into a deal with the London Hydraulic Power Company, on 3rd February, for the provision of hydraulic power day and night at Waterloo Station undertaking to use it only for motive power. Because of both existing congestion, and in anticipation of increased passenger volumes though electric working, further widening of approach lines to the station took place in 1916. Undertaken and completed between Waterloo and Queens Road East Box the widening gave eight tracks, all electrified on the 600v d.c. system, as far as Loco Junction and seven from there to Queens Road. The war did however scale back the planned electrification of the Guildford section to only go as far as Claygate which route went live on 20th November 1916. The decision to use the third-rail system was primarily about operational costs and the need on the suburban services for improvement and acceleration, and to some extent the tight clearances on sections throughout the L&SWR permanent way.

The new Platform 12 of 20th August 1916 was followed a week later by the new Platform 13 and, later that year on 29th October the new Platform 14. The Windsor Line was also further developed when the Booking Office there was opened on 22nd July 1918.

Despite all the changes, be they civilians with umbrellas or Tommies with short Lee-Enfields, Waterloo could in the words of a later war "take it". The Kaiser and the German General Staff couldn't and peace finally returned in 1918, with Waterloo having played a vital part in the British war effort. From enemy action Waterloo suffered some blown out panes of glass from the canopy caused by an explosion on the down main line between Westminster Bridge Road and the A box, as well as No 6 siding on the westerly side of the Windsor Lines. Both incidents were as a result of a German air-raid on 29th September 1917 - one of only 108 such raids in the whole of Great Britain.

CHAPTER FOUR

Interwar years

An LSWR 0-6-0 395 Class locomotive at Waterloo on 10 April 1920. The 395 was in service from 1881 to 1959.

It was Walker's belief that passengers did not relish perusing timetables and preferred the idea of trains leaving at regular intervals, beginning one of the most significant moves in rationalising "the Waterloo of Jerome K. Jerome". Walker extended this time-tabling principle to the outer (main-line) steam services creating standard departure times for those routes and significantly adding thereby to the organisation of the station. The manifestation of this timetable rationalisation on the station itself was the regular allocation of platforms in the rebuilt station. Main-line arrivals were usually set to arrive at Platforms 13 and 14 for example, which in turn made it easier to send empty rolling stock to the yard at Clapham, via the Windsor Lines. Waterloo Station being a significant commuter station had long to deal with the problem of needing significant rolling stock to cope with the demand for peak-times; whereas during the off-peak part of the day services could, and did, run on less stock meaning storage was always needed for units that stood idle for large parts of the day. To an extent this is true of all termini, London land being so costly it was ruinous to store locomotives or rolling stock in extensive and expensive yards near any terminus. However Waterloo with a huge reliance on short-haul suburban passenger traffic had marshalling problems to a greater extent than many stations and that was why the operation of the station was always tied in with satellite yards and sidings.

Works to the roof were not a wartime priority but post-war work on it extended to make a connection with the retained roof structure over the Windsor Lines. The decision to retain the Windsor Lines roof was largely for cost-saving, but also because Walker was concerned about building works inter-acting with peak-hour congestion from the increasing number of tube passengers emerging at that end of the concourse. It was probably an unintentional consequence of retaining the old roof that a vacant space between Platforms 15 and 16 was created.

In what seems to have been a return to the old Waterloo Victorian zeitgeist something had to be done with "the land that had been such a by-product of a casual departure from adherence to central master-planning and, with the war over, building offices became acceptable again. In 1919 a staff block incorporating the stationmaster's office was built on the area of land which had become known to railwaymen as "The Village". Building a village did not mean "The Drain" was forgotten. Having been ordered from America in 1914, escalators were installed leading from "The Drain" to the concourse and situated at the concourse end of The Village, being built either side of the staircase to the subway that hitherto accessed the tube stations. Opened on 9th April 1919, and supplied by Wayford-Otis, the 26' drop meant breaking through the supporting arches of the former North Station, duly replaced with concrete embedded girders, but the ever thrifty L&SWR had the mechanism encased using the skills of their own carriage works.

The iconic main clock at Waterloo Station was also erected in 1919, providing the classic rendez-vous point. A four-sided behemoth suspended from the roof, because the Synchronome system dispenses with workings the clock forms a lighter and hollow square which, whilst de rigeur in today's digital battery age was as much a talking point as a meeting point back in the day.

Refreshments however continued to concern the railway, the thought of Virginia Water residents facing a long walk to a watering hole was unconscionable! An ornate and large buffet was built behind the suburban booking office conveniently located near the infinitely more genteel Windsor Tea Room both of which were opened during 1921.

Having reached the end of the station the Engineering and Estates Committee of 20th February 1919 entertained the proposal to cap works off with a Victory Arch over the steps that led from the York Road to the Windsor Line. Architecturally imposing, the Arch was clearly a response to the War, such a grand entrance would more properly have fitted in with the centre of the station but it was a response to unforeseen events – events which caused the deaths of 585 L&SWR employees during the war. Because the Arch was so significant, both aesthetically and emotionally, Queen Mary officially opened the entire station at that point on 21st March 1922. Both the King and Queen had been due to perform the ceremony but the King had contracted a chill and the day was a cold one. The Arch contains the names of all employees who died in the Kaiser's war the memorial tablets being bronze with ivory enamelled letters, along with the memorial window in cast iron and bronze were made by The Birmingham Guild Ltd (inc Hart-Son-Pecard & Co Ltd), of Berners Street London.

J.W. Jacomb Hood and the equally delightfully named Alfred Weeks Szlumper were not the only ones involved in the design of the new terminus. So James Robb Scott, who eventually become

In 1957 Judy Garland used Waterloo to catch the boat train for Southampton to get the Queen Mary to New York.

Chief Architect at the Southern Railway, and had designed the decorative architectural features of the main frontage block also designed the monumental baroque Victory Arch. A flamboyant display of Portland Stone and bronze, spanning 28' and approximately opposite Platforms 18 and 19 the Arch was surely designed to reflect, if not compete with, the nearby County Hall. Designed to incorporate the L&SWR's war memorial, the arch also represented the culmination of a very lengthy reconstruction programme which took Waterloo from a monument to laissez-faire to a streamlined and efficient station.

More than two decades in construction the complete new station project had cost £2,269,354 to build. Although Hood had died in 1914 his successor, Szlumper, completed the job to deliver what was the first new London terminus of the Twentieth Century. Arguably Waterloo was also the best laid out London terminus, capable of handling the enormous volume of commuters inherent on being the busiest station in the metropolis, as well as holiday traffic without the need for complicated rearrangements. At this point Waterloo was handling around 1,000 trains a day requiring 1,400 signal movements in a station covering an area of 24 1/2 acres, which had involved over 500,000 square yards of "Asphalte" works. The roof at Waterloo required some 60 miles of glazing bars weighing around 95 tons, which supported some 25,000 glass panes weighing approximately 1,000 tons, all based on the "Invincible" system of Messrs W Edgecumbe Rendell & Co (Victoria Street Westminster), and measured 520' x 540' with a maximum single span of 118'.

CHAPTER FIVE

The triumphal tour of Waterloo

As a by-product of all the station developments, the new Waterloo reclaimed the title as Britain's biggest railway station from Edinburgh Waverley. However, what was the station actually like? What was the monument built? Starting along the concourse from opposite Platform 1 and progressing to Platform 21 our imaginary stroll would show:-

A generously sized cloakroom some 60' long capable of dealing with projections of 295,000 items a year situated opposite Platforms 1

An LSWR 4-4-0 pulls a passenger train out of Waterloo in the 1920. Note the plethroa of signals at this date.

to 3. This cloakroom had additional storage space in the basement and adjoining arches underneath it these being accessed by a lift within the cloakroom. These units were large enough to keep ocean luggage on the barrows thereby speeding up handling times (and reducing costs).

The entrance to the gentlemen's toilets, or "Gentlemen's Court" as the L&SWR addressed the difficult social issue of terminology, is, opposite Platform 3 down an intermediate flight of stairs. Whilst the Ladies' lavatories were perhaps a trifle perfunctory, albeit divided into First-Class and Third-Class, the Gentleman's were an altogether different affair. Perhaps reflecting the role of Waterloo as such a suburban station dealing with commuters, still perforce mainly male workers, the Gentlemen had no class distinction but instead reflected a massive homage to male needs. The subterranean facilities for male travellers measured some 800' long and 40' wide with marble floors of black and white tiles, and white glazed "Victorian" fireclay tiles on the walls lending it a clean and fresh look. Amongst the facilities for male travellers in this, what "The Railway Magazine" suggested was "perhaps the finest [convenience] in London" were boot-cleaning facilities, bathrooms, an hairdressing salon and of course the lavatories, supplied by Shanks. With sanitary fittings supplied by the nearby Doulton works and tiles from the Leeds Fireclay Company (who supplied many of the other tiles throughout the station) the clean white lines were offset by a terracotta feature which gave the impression of being marble, although the promotional adverts suggested the lavatory basins came with "St. Ann's" marble tops and friezes.

Indeed it is worth commenting that when the L&SWR entered into a deal with the Trustees of Faulkener's hairdressers the range of fittings was extensive and of high quality. Display cases were mahogany, as was the counter and the frames around the plate glass mirrors. The Saloon on the south side of the concourse included four shampoo basins set in a white marble block 21' x 172x 1 ¼" with 10" high marble splashbacks, and four plate glass mahogany framed mirrors each 4' 9" x3'. The lavatory and bath rooms included 12 basins with hot and cold water set in a marble shelf surmounted by eight plate glass mirrors with brush and comb shelves underneath; three bathrooms each containing a porcelain enamelled iron bath 6' 322 x 2' 7 ½". The Hairdressing Saloon south side extension included the 14' 1" x 1' 11" range of three shampoo lavatories with polished Sicilian marble top matched by three recessed fronted white basins with a 12" marbled skirting, four electric lights, two points for electric hair brushes and a gas fire.

The hairdressing saloon on the North side of the concourse had the range of four shampoo basins in polished marble top and plated fittings, two mahogany show cases 7' x 6' 2", and although clocks were part of all the specifications here one was specifically a Synchronome clock – nothing was to be left to chance when it came to catching trains. The lavatory bath rooms and dressing rooms had two ranges of lavatory basins each 15' long with marble skirting and front, each fitted with five basins, plated fittings and accompanied by mahogany framed mirrors. There were six dressing rooms each fitted with a white porcelain lavatory basin on plated supports, with plated fittings and towel rail, hot and cold water, plate glass mirror 2' 6" x 1' 6" with a glass shelf underneath a hat rail with two brass hooks and an electric light with shade and switch. There were three bathrooms each fitted with a porcelain enamelled iron bath , plated fittings, lavatory basin, heated towel rail, mirror and glass shelf, hat rail with two brass hooks, glazed pedestal WC and an electric light with shade and switch. Interestingly such grandeur was not extended to the attendant's room which had two painted hat rails with nine iron hooks, a cupboard so bland it was not specified, but did have the electric light with shade and switch!

Adjacent to the short flight of stairs leading down to the Gentlemen's Court was another leading up to the General Offices above.

Opposite Platform 4 to just before Platform 6 was a Luggage Hall generally of similar proportions to the Cloakroom being 75' x45'. If anything symbolised the new L&SWR desire for organisation it was the Luggage Hall that was accessible from the concourse, the cab yard and the adjacent Booking Hall. Self-evident it may be that function should inform architectural form but hitherto nothing in the L&SWR's history at Waterloo (Bridge) had given any hint of awareness of such a principle!

The Booking Hall, to the north-west of the Luggage Hall, was very Edwardian in style built with plaster columns supporting a very plain but curved ceiling. Being 95' long, 45' wide, and 30' high the Booking Hall was commodious and airy, containing half the elliptical teak Booking Office (the other half was on the concourse itself eventually being demolished by British Rail in 1971) and had parquet floors. However in 1924 this room was modernised – the plaster columns were replaced with Breche marble columns having bronze caps in the Roman Doric style; whilst the floor became coloured glass tiles. The Booking Hall also had the access to the cab yard removed when the doors thereto were replaced by windows.

The Booking Hall also gave access to a general waiting room, itself also accessible from the concourse; however the Ladies' First-Class waiting room which was tucked behind this one was, in the interests of their protection, only accessible from the Booking Hall. Conversely the Third-Class Ladies waiting room, which was adjacent to the First-Class, was only accessible from the concourse! Toilet provision for ladies was also segregated but both facilities abutted each other and were located adjacent to their respective waiting rooms.

Next along the concourse were the stairs and lifts to the upstairs Surrey Room whilst

The Duke of Wellington, who defeated Napoelon at Waterloo, lived long enough to use the station.

further along the concourse was a Refreshment Buffet. The Refreshment Buffet had an outer wall broadly of the same dimensions as the Cloakroom and Luggage Hall but, being located in the inner radius of the concourse curve, had a smaller frontage which may have informed the decision to give a circular interior design with a semi-circular buffet counter against the cab yard wall. With small circular tables for passenger's comfort, they could eat amongst the many marble hues that adorned the walls, with Roman style mosaic marble floor.

At this point we might have been stunned so choose to go upstairs for a quick break. In the same block which contained the Booking Hall, but located upstairs, was the Surrey Dining Room. Also accessed by marble stairs and a lift the Surrey Room, opposite Platform 11, had coupled columns supporting the staircase ceiling; the room itself panelled in English oak after the Georgian style, with leaded windows overlooking both the station and the approach road. In the Surrey Room which was intended for commercial hire in the evenings, and could seat 150, a grill was located in the corner, and behind a screened recess meals were sent down from the kitchen above. Adjacent to the Surrey Room was a much smaller ladies' tea-room that did light luncheons and a tea service.

Now, in our imaginary perambulation, we have reached the wide and, when passing through the office block, lofty passage which allowed a generously proportioned cab road, with pavements at either side, giving access to the station, between Platforms 11 and 12, from the cab yard access that ran just outside the station. The cab road passes under the office block with an enormous leaded-glass window displaying the coat of arms of the L&SWR and carved in stone relief the names of counties served by the Company. Although the reliefs were always visible to anyone with an eye to see, their height above ground meant some could not appreciate them from close-up, which is now possible with the creation of the new shopping level in the Twenty-first century.

On the concourse the Luggage Hall opposite the loading bay for Platform 12, was only accessible from the concourse because to the rear of it was another set of stairs, and a lift, to the General Offices above. This small entrance was followed by a further Luggage Hall some three-quarters of the size of that opposite Platform 4 et seq.

Passing the Luggage Hall we see a second protuberance from the almost Nash-style crescent radius: the new Booking Office, which contained windows A-H. Unlike the Booking Hall opposite Platforms 6 to 9 this one is entirely on the concourse and forms only a semi-circle because it fronts another Refreshment Buffet accessed from doors located either side of the Booking Hall. However this Refreshment Buffet is rectangular, 79' by 39' with an ornamental plaster ceiling 18' high, and the server here being adjacent to the side of the cab road. Externally advertised by white art-nouveau letters on blue mosaics the buffet signs little prepare one for the riot of rich baroque within. With panelled marble extending up 9', panels of rouge marble were inserted in the upper plaster walls and surmounted by Grinling Gibbons-style ornamentation of drooping swags over the marble-work, introduced some colour. The walls contained Greek cipollino and statuary bays some 11' tall; the pilasters were in the fluted sienna style the adjoining columns in Greek cipollino with bronze caps and bases.

Next to this Refreshment Room, and opposite "The Village", was another tea-room soon to be named "the Windsor Room". With cream walls, extensive mirrors, a floor of polished oak parquet, and fittings of mahogany the Windsor Room was clearly aspiring to stimulate Royal patronage for the Royal residents in the Royal Town within the Royal County. The Windsor Room consciously harked back to the Edwardian age with fluted pilasters atop columns in shades of grey and white with two domed pay-boxes containing curved glass windows either side of the door.

Adjacent to the Windsor Tea Room, but for only some 2/3 of the depth was the Third-Class Ladies' waiting room, itself adjacent to a similar depth Ladies' First Class waiting room, itself next to a general waiting room. Behind all these rooms the remaining 1/3 of the depth was occupied by extensive lavatory accommodation exclusively for ladies and accessed directly from their waiting rooms; although only the First Class ladies had bath and dressing rooms. The Gentlemen here had to go underground to another "Gentlemen's Court" accessed from the concourse approximately opposite Platform 16 and adjacent to the general Waiting Room.

Because the original cloakroom on the station had handled some 41,000 items or so a year a new and more generously sized provision is the next sight on our journey and forms the last room before the Victory Arch, which latter gives access to the station from the York Road.

We now reach the Victory Arch its sheer splendour, when viewed from outside, makes it more of a statement than the main entrance over the central cab-way (which latter, significantly, is also the only place where the General Office block rises to a fourth storey).

Critics have called the Victory Arch "overblown" but study of the drawings and model, produced before the decision was taken to make what was always going to be an "arched entrance" the "Victory Arch", shows that the addition of statuary and, of course, the names was the most significant change. It is perhaps best to regard Scott's own words:

"The sculptural decorations are three groups, two of which are semi-circular in composition, placed on pylons either side of the arch. The one on the left, representing War 1914, has a central figure of Bellona, Goddess of war, wild and distraught, clad in scaled armour, astride the world, with a flaming torch and naked sword dealing death and destruction. The other, on the right, representing Peace, 1919, has for its motive a figure of peace seated and enthroned upon the earth, and holding a palm branch and a small figure of winged victory, symbolic of peace with Victory, bringing abundance and contentment whilst commerce and liberal arts flourish. The panel around the Arch is decorated with war trophies and discs giving the names of the different countries where our men have fought. The whole is surmounted and finished by the central group of Britannia, seated and triumphant holding aloft the sacred torch of Liberty to her own greatness and glory, and for the guidance of her children and children's children and the benefit of mankind in general."

Resuming our imaginary stroll an arch clearly must have two sides and on the other side of the Victory Arch is the entrance to the General Offices with a lift in a hall protected by a porter's office and from which a corridor also gained access to the retained former General Offices now imaginatively renamed: "The Old General Offices". Next to this was the entrance to the City and Underground railways - but wait! We have left our tightly furled umbrella behind in the cloakroom opposite Platform 1 we must proceed with haste to regain it but with time to admire the platforms and "The Village" as well as a few joys in the central concourse.

At the end of Platform 20 to 21 is a site for some shops which need not detain us, the wooden train indicator at the ends of Platform 18 to 19 may catch our eye as a fine example of a locally produced mechanism by the Company and looking to our left we see a vertical stand containing train timetables, the first item in the central spine running down the concourse. We reach Platforms 16 and 17 marvelling at the banks of telephones staring at the WH Smith bookstall on the central spine.

We have now reached "The Village" and stairs/escalators to "The Drain" which, had we time to go down, we would see decorated by a series of oil paintings being part of the advertisement campaign for the British Dominions Insurance Company. At a glance we realise here, above ground, is the Lost Property Office, but we are unaware that this handles all lost items on the railway network that can lead to 40-50,000 items a year. We also notice the flower and fruit stall but may not be aware that "The Village" also contains, at ground floor, the stationmaster's public offices (his clerk and his private rooms being directly above), and a cluster of mess rooms for the GPO, travelling post sorters, policemen, porters as well as pay offices. On the first-floor of "The Village" are a guard's room and a large dining room with its own kitchen - this feeds the clerks employed at the station and in the General Offices.

Nothing catches our eye as we approach the central cab road other than the stairs down to Waterloo Road located on the central concourse spine so we cross the cab road and find W.H. Smith have

A preserved LSWR passenger coach sporting its livery of black, brown and salmon pink. (James E. Petts)

an even larger bookstall on the central spine, opposite Platform 11 and just beyond Platform 10, both of which platforms have telephone boxes. At the end of Platform 8 and 9 is an Inquiries section helpfully located opposite more stairs down to Waterloo Road. Another, and larger, indicator for trains is at the end of Platforms 6 and 7, and we regard more timetables on the central spine opposite the midway point between Platforms 5 and 6. Another bookstall at the ends of Platform 4 and 5, a tobacconist at the end of Platform 3 adjacent to a place for ticket examiners at Platform 2 and as we turn to the cloakroom we just have time to notice the inspector's facility at the end of Platform 1. Stunned at this station, this paean to modernity we note up against the end wall the final item on the central spine a show case as, just in time we regain our comfortingly British and suburban umbrella.

A quick glance at the big picture shows us the concourse connects and unites all passenger facilities. Light and airy, and destined to largely escape the pall of London smoke and intense steam locomotive working for over half a century it also looks clean and spacious with a hint of modernity. Serving all platforms the concourse is 770' long, 120' wide, and also includes an inquiry office. The original plan had been to make it straight, drawing the commencement of the "Windsor" lines to a point roughly where the Victory Arch was. However the decision to broadly retain the original station meant the concourse itself had to be adapted and while this gives a pleasing aspect to the brick wall of the office block it may be argued that it denies the station of the cohesion originally intended. By not only having a separate station needing accommodations of roof style, retaining Khartoum contributed to a sense of isolation from the rest of the station. Certainly, as a regular user, given that I had easy access to the Tubes or the Victory Arch to get me to the beating heart of the metropolis, and coupled with the fact you could not see the whole station, there was never really a sense of awareness of its totality. It probably worked in reverse too with other users being unaware of our little piece of the station.

Under the concourse are two subways one above the other. The lowest subway is an operating preserve of the railway and starts, at street level, from Griffin Street near the milk roadway and extends to the parcels office, rather appropriately since the subway's purpose is for parcels and luggage. The parcels subway can be accessed from nine lifts in the new station and one at Khartoum. Above the parcels subway is another one intended for citizens and supplies an alternative means of going from platform to platform also enabling transfer to the tube. This subway extends from Platform 1 to the incline for "The Drain" just to the west of the station, and can be accessed from all platforms save 16 to 21.

We are not aware this station, at time of opening, was under Mr Jerrett the stationmaster who, with his three Assistant Stationmasters, was by now responsible for a railway staff of 450 - which totally excludes staff located in the general offices and those in all the many refreshment facilities. Messrs Spiers & Pond Limited, reassuringly the owners and operators of the Criterion Grill and who had originally started in Australia by providing the refreshments for railway travellers between Melbourne and the gold-rush town of Ballarat in the 1850s, operated the refreshment facilities.

Had Mr Jerrett the time he would tell us that, having assessed the architecture, it is only right to consider the actual platforms - the raison d'être for the new station. There were 13 platforms, eight of which had two faces, and 21 platform lines. The first platform was double-sided serving No 1 line (696') for services to Hampton Court and No 2 also for local services such as Leatherhead (695'). Platform No3 (683') for Shepperton services, and No4 (685') for Kingston lines are similarly separated by a double-sided platform but along this one stood the supporting pillars for the first span of the roof. The same double-sided platform arrangement applies to lines 5 (720') and 6 (723') these lines being generally allocated for various specials, routine boat trains to Southampton and race trains; as well as 7 (728') for Bournemouth and 8 (735') for Portsmouth but this platform contains the columns for the second span. Lines 9 (756') and 10 (765'), generally for miscellaneous main-line stopping routes to country stations are served by a double-sided platform whereas line 11 (860' later extended to 946') for trains of special length, usually the principal boat trains, is accessed by a single platform with the cab yard alongside on which were also the columns supporting the third arch. Approximately a third of the way down each of the newly built platforms was a flight of steps leading on to an 18' wide subway that provided access to the two tube stations underneath Waterloo. Each of the new platforms also had an electric lift that accessed the tunnel beneath the pedestrian one thereby allowing the railway to move luggage, mail and parcels throughout the station without interfering with the passengers. Alas such consideration was long gone by the 'sixties, when passengers were immured to being corralled by long parcel units snaking in wide arcs on the concourse itself.

Between lines 11 and 12 there is an extensive cab yard accessed via a ramp up from York Road and in such a manner the cab drew in, in the same direction as an arriving train. Two short loading docks (of 160' and 175') are located at the end of the cab yard furthest away from the concourse, and formed the only sidings under the station roof.

As line 11 is served by a single-sided platform so it was with line 12 (843') generally loading mail, parcels and available for other non-passenger use although it could be used for arrivals, and it too had supporting pillars this time for the fourth span. Lines 13 (857') and 14 (at 860' and, along with Platform 11, the longest) were served by a double-sided platform. Conversely 15 (635') fed into a single-sided platform and carried the supports for the fifth roof-span being fenced off at the non-track side with the access to the parcels office and manager's office being on the other side of the fence. Lines 13 to 15 were usually used for main-line arrivals for trains not scheduled to turn round for an outgoing service although luggage, parcels, the milk trains and even a reasonable amount of fish usually brought in by road from the north London termini also departed from 15.

Of the 21 platform lines: 1 to 6 and 16 to 21 inclusive were for electric traction, 11 was mainly for boat train departures, 12 to 15 were for main-line arrivals; 1 to 15 had direct access to the subway for the tube and all except 16, 18, 21 had luggage lifts.

Naturally enough the sixth and final roof-span was atypical since it had to conjoin two different roofs but, overall, the roof is a wondrous expanse of glass although noticeably a return to the "ridge and

The hydraulic buffers, seen here on a 1930s cigarette card, are still in place at Waterloo.

furrow" style of construction rather than a large single span arch, or even a series of them. Nine spans at right-angles to the tracks covered Platforms 1 to 15, the ridges 60' above the platforms and 25 spans parallel with the rails were over the concourse. Although a station for the new century, the engineering costs meant the roof consciously harked back to the style and construction of an earlier age, rather than the grandeur of a single-span arch, such as at St Pancras, because the other costs in running a railway had greatly increased the proportion of overheads to income. At this period typically railway operating costs in relation to the gross operating revenue were of the order of 80-85% whereas in the 1840's the L&SWR was showing 43%.

The remaining platforms, under the 1885 Victorian roof, were a single-sided Platform 16 (570'), for Wimbledon via East Putney and Shepperton via Richmond followed by a double-sided platform serving lines 17 (600'), for Hounslow via Richmond and 18 (612') Hounslow via Brentford. These were followed by another double-sided platform for lines 19 (605') serving the Kingston loop, and 20 (625'). Line 21 (551') was served by a platform but to all intents and purposes was the final operational suburban platform, being used along with 20 for the Windsor and Reading routes despite there being a short 234'platform beyond serving a de facto line 22 ordinarily intended for loading vans although, by the time of my own trips to London I can recall arriving there at various times.

Waterloo was, we would have been told, now no longer an open station because platforms had Bostwick gates within artistic iron screens installed across the entrances from Platforms 1 to 15; gates for Platforms 16 to 21 would follow later. There was however no desire or attempt to block the cab access between 11 and 12.

Beyond the westernmost platform, outside the station walls, remained the space for carriage sidings, coaling facilities, turntable and engine sidings. No longer spacious enough to accommodate all the demand at Waterloo, some accommodation for engine and carriage sidings served by a turntable, was located on the Down side immediately on the other side of Westminster Bridge Road.

CHAPTER SIX

The wonder of Waterloo

Daily train service usage, at the time of opening Waterloo Station, amounted to electric trains with 175 arrivals under the new roof and 176 under the old roof; with 176 and 180 departures respectively. Steam traction formed 129 arrivals under the new roof with 38 under the old one; complemented by departures of 129 and 39 respectively. The railway claimed to handle more than 140,000 passengers a day which, with 52 empty trains arriving, 65 empty

In June 1967 two of the last steam locomotives prepare to leave Waterloo with the then new Shell Centre behind.

trains departing and assorted mail/freight trains, the L&SWR happily promoted their daily total for a 24-hour period was some 1,159 trains. The Company was at great pains to remind people that that total could rise to 1,370 a day in the summer when taking into account race meetings, summer excursions, specials and some specials even at night. In their promotional literature the L&SWR pointed out that during the period of construction they built a station and catered to the needs of some 750 million passengers from some 5 million trains.

It was no surprise therefore, following railway "rationalisation", in 1922, that when the L&SWR morphed into the Southern Railway (SR) Waterloo became the flagship station of the new company. An early change under SR was the arrival of the National Provincial Bank, in January 1924, the first bank on a British station. Another early impact from the new company at the station was somewhat minor when, on 3rd May 1925, the remains of the SER connecting line near the Junction at Waterloo station were finally removed thereby expunging a chequered part of Waterloo's history.

The pace of change involving locomotives and other traction units used at Waterloo was increasing with the rolling out of electrification to Guildford and Leatherhead on 12th July 1925 meaning that steam traction was no longer a day-time feature on Platforms 1 to 5. The Southern had, however, not entirely abandoned steam traction embarking on a new engine building programme for their long-distance services. The SR, in 1925, introduced the "King Arthur" class named with an eye to the Devon and Somerset traffic; and, in 1926, the "Lord Nelson" class, named after famous Admirals to appeal to the Channel ports traffic. Walker was far from unaware of the importance of marketing or advertising, introducing the "Atlantic Coast Express" as a nomenclature for the 11a.m. service, the principal one of those during the day, to the West of England.

From 13th September 1926 the London Electric Railway Company (LER) brought a third tube to Waterloo Station and this one connected it to three other London termini. Later known as the Northern Line the extension from Charing Cross to Kennington passed through Waterloo and gave a direct connection to Euston and, with only one change the Kings Cross/St Pancras termini.

On 8th July 1927 the LER, notified the Ministry of Transport "the Up escalator at Waterloo will be completed and ready for inspection by the 27th inst" and by the 21st were actively pressing for the inspection. On the 26h July the LER sent revised drawings showing the escalator emerging approximately under Platforms 19 and 20 of the L&SWR, with the LER booking hall floor extending under Platform 16 of the Waterloo terminus. Accordingly the Ministry authorised Colonel Mount to inspect the works on Wednesday morning 27th July and he wrote his Report on the 28th July. Essentially, in their totality, the works inspected comprised a triple escalator tunnel, with internal dimensions of 22' 4", designed to connect the Southern Railway's passenger subway, which passed transversely under Waterloo Station, with the passages at the bottom of the existing four lifts installed to access the platforms of the Bakerloo and Hampstead lines. The escalators were some of the deepest in the country extending 56' 3" made up of 212 steps 84 of which were exposed on the slope and a length of level treads at the top of 6'. Each escalator was expected to accommodate a maximum of 170 passengers at a time and travel at 100' a minute.

Colonel Mount had reservations about the brake capacity but was assured that trials were being carried out with stronger springs at Clapham South however he recommended approval whilst also drawing attention of the Southern Railway to the potential that the increased volume of LER passengers may prove to be too great for the SR's own escalators. On 9th August the Southern Railway acknowledged the letter of 29th July from the Ministry, "...this question is being carefully considered by our departmental officers, but it is thought desirable that this matter should be held in abeyance until we have had some experience of the effect of the alterations......"

By 3rd October 1927 the LER could again write to the Ministry "...the second and third escalators will be completed by the 10th instant, and ready for inspection. The work comprises certain alterations to the structure of the Southern Railway for the provision of Booking Offices etc., and as arranged with that Company". On 6th Oct the LER were advised Col Mount would inspect on Tuesday 11th at 10a.m and the Report recommending, "that this triple escalator installation be finally approved for traffic, subject to the completion of the minor works, and to future decision in respect of the adequacy of the facilities afforded by the Southern Railway escalators when sufficient experience of the effect of the altered arrangements has been gained" was typed the same day. A representative from Southern Railway also attended this inspection. These works for approval were essentially two escalators not yet brought into use, with a passimeter (a turnstile operated from inside a change booth that gives access to a public transportation area) and a booking office. The Booking Office was at the head of the escalator tunnel, on the paved concourse but formed between two of the viaduct arches under Waterloo Station.

In 1928 the Post Office (London) Railway from Paddington to the eastern sorting office at Whitechapel was finally opened. Decided on in 1911, tunnel boring did not begin until 1915 and the war slowed matters with track laying commencing in 1924. Dubbed "Mail Rail" the driverless trains running on a 2' gauge 70' below the streets of London in 9' diameter tunnels was a great success. Plans to connect Mail Rail to Waterloo Kings Cross, Euston, Cannon Street, and London Bridge did not materialise and connections to this delightful line, closed on 30th May 2003, were by mail van from mail trains arriving at Waterloo.

In 1929 SR marked the fact that the journey to Bournemouth was now back to two hours by the naming of the "Bournemouth Limited" train. Residents of Bournemouth were further courted in 1931 when the "Bournemouth Belle" was introduced providing a prestigious all-Pullman service. If suburban services were a mainstay at Waterloo – glamour and cache was to be found at the long-haul runs.

However if new trains were coming on stream others were going. The last a.c. powered trains ran on 22nd September 1929 by which time all a.c. lines were powered by d.c. Interestingly 1929 was also the year that the railways were given powers to operate air services – something the Southern actively pursued.

An aviation activity the Southern could not engage in was the Schneider Cup seaplane races which, in 1929, saw the Southern swing into action carrying people to Spithead again, and kept Waterloo engaged more happily than MPs seeking en masse trips!. Train timetable changes were minor but certainly on 7th and 8th September demand caused suspension of seat reservations and cancellations of any restaurant cars usually provided on certain trains.

At least there was some sense to the Southern's understanding of how aviation could impact on them. How the newly rebuilt roof came to be considered as an aerodrome for aircraft to literally impact on the Southern's Waterloo Station must count as one of the more bizarre aspects in the station's history. Following a Cabinet Minute of 6th November 1929 an investigation into the practicality of an aerodrome over the new Charing Cross Station was authorised and, should that be unviable, then to look at other stations as well as a scheme "to erect an aerodrome over the new Charing Cross Station and Waterloo Station combined"! The Waterloo feasibility calculated a cost of £5million involving covering streets ("open to objection from an architectural point of view") and which the railway company felt also to be undesirable ("would greatly depreciate the value of properties in the neighbourhood"). Quite what pilots would have thought of landing through the steam from the Bournemouth Express was seemingly never solicited. In a classic piece of dry understatement on 9th December 1929 the engineer to the Southern Railway, G Elson, commented; "There would be great difficulty in finding sites for suitable supports to the proposed Aerodrome owing to the existence of the railway tracks and platforms of Waterloo Station and the Tube Stations underneath"

Back on terra firma, the Windsor Line was electrified on 6th July 1930, leaving the only steam trains in the North Station being those supplying the Reading services, and by which time thirty-two electric trains left Waterloo during the evening peak, then classified as 5 to 6

Queen Elizabeth and the Duke of Edinburgh first used Waterloo together on their honeymoon in 1947.

pm. Indeed by the 1930s Waterloo was adapting to all-electric suburban commuter services as well as the main line into Portsmouth. Steam was now to be found only on long-distance services to the south coast and the West Country with the last services ironically finishing on 9th July 1967 when the Kinks were at number two in the charts with "Waterloo Sunset", and No 35030 brought the last steam train into Waterloo thereby ending 119 years of steam traction. However reduced the role of steam may have been it was still the service seen to have the most caché. Nobody has yet branded a commuter train the "Bracknell Bullet" or the "Esher Express". The Southern had not forsaken their formative era and were running ocean-liner expresses to Southampton docks making sure that the prestigious Pullman cars were included amongst the carriages that made up those expresses.

Whatever the traction, passengers often needed guidance and Waterloo was a pioneer in the use of loudspeakers they were certainly in use in 1932, being first used on 9th March – a day when Waterloo had to cope with a clash between a rugger international at Twickenham and the Boat Race. Whilst the acoustics and the enunciation made clarity variable it did reflect the start of something new and a tacit recognition that passenger volumes were increasing enough that flexibility and interactivity were needed, Hamilton Ellis saying the trigger was football crowds. During Hitler's war it was not unknown to play uplifting music over the loudspeakers as well. To accommodate loudspeaker provision the announcer's office was initially located in booth over a kiosk situated approximately opposite Platforms 8 and 9 (but later in a glass "bubble" atop the stationmaster's office in "The Village" and now part of the new control room accessed from stairs off Platform 1).

Communications and media at Waterloo was not confined to loudspeakers for on 27th August 1934 along the entrance and concourse wall of Platform 1 above the approach road near the same platform the Southern Railway instigated a News Cinema. With a 250 seat capacity and erected on girders to allow it to continue over the cab road, the front of the cinema was very a la mode being in the jazz style being designed by Alistair Macdonald – son of the far from style trendy Labour Leader Ramsay. The point of the cinema was to show programmes in one-hour cycles, where the cycle would show cartoons, topical feature-ettes, and news films.

The tradition of renaming stations within the wider Waterloo area was not yet dead. On 7th July 1935 Waterloo Junction was renamed as – "Waterloo Eastern"! However in at least one attempt to avoid a return to confusion the four platform faces at Waterloo Eastern became A-D.

Whether lettered or numbered platforms, tracks occupy a small part of our story, but are pivotal to the running of a station. A feat across 16th-17th May 1936 deserves mention both for engineering prowess and demonstrating the employment significance of the railways. The approach roads again needed an operational modification to accompany the conversion to electric running, all electric trains approaching Platforms 1 to 6 had only one approach road, and such changes meant amended colour light signalling. During just seven hours of this night some 1000 workmen carried out the necessary work on the approach roads to ensure no disruption to the heavy commuter services. The result of the works, part of a £500,000 programme, on Waterloo Station included the rerouting of various approach roads and the electrification of Platforms 7 to 9.

Signal changes needed at the terminus were delayed until the end of the holiday season and although signalling is ancillary to our story some reference needs to be made to a little regarded building just outside Waterloo. Opened on 18th October 1936, the first train under electric signalling being the newspaper train for Yeovil departing at 1.30 a.m., the new power signalling box looked sleek and modern with smooth uncluttered art deco lines. This signal box was the biggest the Southern Railway built: a unique design which was built almost entirely of concrete, and located on the site of the former blacksmiths shop at the west side of the station throat. While the staff commanded a view from the first floor, the ground floor provided the relay room with accommodation for the signal maintenance staff as well as stores and a small workshop. With three frames and 309 levers (although the working lever total was only 282: made up of 77 for points, 203 for coloured light signals two special levers and 27 spare), 153 track circuits and 16 train describers the new signal box replaced all the mechanical boxes. The relatively modest little signal box allowed the extension of the electrification so vital to Walker's vision.

With the full station having been operational for some 15 years it was decided, in 1937, that the provision for waiting and luggage space had been over-generous. The Waiting Room opposite Platforms 8 and 9 became an Inquiry office and part of the Luggage Hall opposite Platforms 12 and 13 became the Post Office.

During 1937, in stages, the main-line to Portsmouth was electrified (completed on 4th July) as were the lines to Alton and Chertsey. This meant at Waterloo that the main-line Platforms, 7 to 15, were fitted with the third-rail thereby completing the electrification of the terminus although the roll out of electric services was still not complete across the Southern Railway network. Platforms 7, 8, and 11 were lengthened; while, on Platforms 9 to 14, the comfort of passengers was maintained, at the price of some diminution in aestheticism, by erecting umbrella awnings all of which extended beyond the station roof.

CHAPTER SEVEN

World War 2

Significant when The Great War began, Waterloo was as vital for the following generation, although this time the building itself was expected to be a target and, as a result, the Bodmin & Wadebridge carriage was moved to the subway. Photographs also exist of workmen, in 1939, replacing glass on the roof of the station with asbestos sheets. It took until the raid of 7th September 1940 for the station itself to be affected but a bomb in nearby Juxon Street some 2,450 yards down the line from the A Box had a devastating impact.

A South West Trains Class 455 electrical multiple unit, which entered service in 1982. (Chris McKenna)

Above the crater the rails passed with no support having had their piers demolished in the explosion. Arches that supported the Windsor Line Through Up and Down Roads had cracked and shifted off their piers which were also cracked. Waterloo had two local lines which could be used for vans but not passenger trains and the Down Main Through was bent, the station was at a standstill.

The Juxon Street crater was impossible to tackle for 58 hours because of the bomb damage on the line, although the King made a visit on the 9th September. Once the tracks were capable of getting a crane to the point 200 soldiers arrived to start filling in the crater and assist in shoring up the arches with massive timber joists of 18" baulk timber.

The line was not yet operational after the Juxon Street bomb when, on 20th September, with Waterloo spluttering back to life another bomb landed by Doulton's works between Salamanca Street (ironically named after another Wellington victory) and Black Prince Road, causing damage and punching a hole I' in diameter through an arch supporting the Up Main Local line. By the 23rd the "Doulton crater" was filled in, although the Luftwaffe had caused enough damage by then that the Station was paralysed with no working points or signals. Waterloo did not return to full operations until 1st October.

Waterloo continued to take hits and the power station at Durnsford Road, Wimbledon, was hit on the night of 14th October 1940. Although not part of Waterloo Station itself, the impact of the bombed power station was enormous: with one chimney gone and generating capacity reduced by the loss of half the boilers such trains as were running were often on reduced speed.

Automatic signalling was again knocked out on 17th October meaning Waterloo lost control of all routes within 2 ½ miles of the station causing hand signals to be used from people hastily pressed into service – the trained men being few and needed on other duties.

The former L&SWR General Offices were blasted in the incendiary raids of 29th December 1940 a raid leading to fires on the roof of Waterloo and amongst other buildings a nearby rubber factory. In the morning there were many blocked lines and points had to be worked by hand although, by a peculiar irony, one of the few trains that could run easily was the Necropolis train which had been protected from a delayed action bomb by a line of coal wagons.

By 5.30 p.m. on 5th January 1941 the station had normal working but four hours later the station was hit again, destroying the General Manager's Office, and damaging the underground. Already damaged in an earlier raid on this night it was the final death blow for the Old General Offices. Later that year, on 16th April 1941, at the other side of Waterloo, Necropolis' luck ran out as bombing destroyed both their station and the funeral train finally burying that company and service.

As if that was not serious enough the next month, on 10th May, Waterloo was extensively hit again. One incendiary bomb landed near the electric workshop and that of the Building Department blowing doors off and another bomb landing soon thereafter caused extensive damage to some parcel vans (others were moved away in time). The Chairman's car was destroyed as were some other vehicles but more seriously the fire spread to timber in other arches. Bonded spirits, worth £30,000, stored in arches beneath the platforms blazed extensively causing a long closure – rather ironically no doubt creating thirsty work for the firemen. Beginning soon after midnight the fire's impact was compounded by an earlier bomb breaking the water mains in both Waterloo and York Road; the supply of water for steam engines was pumped dry by nine in the morning. "The Drain" lived up to its name with water from its sumps being brought into play by heroic Heath Robinson improvisation and all but the fires in the Bonded warehouse were dealt with, despite the efforts of the Fire Brigade also hosing from the river. The spirits aflame were not quenched until 15th May, thereby allowing partial reopening of the station.

Whilst blacked out trying to avoid German bombs Waterloo was also a test centre for fluorescent lighting installations. The rather ominous sounding Ministry of Home Security, Civil Defence Research Committee, Sub Committee C (Luminescent materials) reported on 16th July 1943 that, in the spring of 1942, experimental equipment was installed by the Southern Railway at Waterloo Station. The purpose of this experiment, and the Report acknowledges the assistance of Mr A Cunnington, the Chief Lighting Engineer of the Southern Railway, was to ascertain "to what extent fluorescent markings could facilitate the movement of passengers during blackout hours, particularly after an 'alert' had been sounded, when all category 'C' lighting would be extinguished and only the very limited category of 'B' lighting would remain in use. It was anticipated that at certain points of special difficulty to passengers, such as staircases, road-crossings etc, fluorescent paint energised by ultra-violet light might be helpful, without contravening the Lighting (Restrictions) Order, 1940"

There were four locations for the lighting experiment. Firstly, the Memorial Arch entrance stairway (which initially had a 100 Watt tungsten lamp and black filter fixed above the steps and fluorescent paint on the handrails and a strip at the side and centre of the steps. Later this became an 80 Watt black-bulb mercury light and strips of luminescent vitreous enamelled metal). Secondly illumination was tested at the stairway adjoining Platform 21 leading to the Bakerloo Line (an 80 Watt black-bulb mercury light and two coats of fluorescent paint on the handrails and strips on the stairs). The third test was at the road crossing on the bridge between Waterloo and Waterloo Eastern (originally with two sets of lighting one with six tungsten lamps with black filters and one with two 80 Watt black-bulb mercury lights; the edge of the crossing, the bottom of the Belisha Beacon and two direction signs treated with fluorescent paint. Later the light fitting was changed to an 80 Watt black-bulb mercury light fitted with an enamelled shade coated with a high fluorescent material – which had been too bright so reduced to a small strip). The final installation was a "telephones sign" under the cab exit which sign was 4' long with 9" letters energised by four 5-Watt argon lamps mounted in a trough.

That the lighting experiments were not an unqualified success may perhaps be judged by the fact the sub-committee concluded, in less than ringing terms, that the materials "are of reasonably good performance".

To borrow from an old song what was it like "underneath the arches" in wartime Waterloo?" Harry Greenfield, Waterloo Station master and son of a guard to Queen Victoria's Royal Train, was also Chief Warden so was also largely responsible for the relationship between Waterloo and the local civilian population. The available arches could accommodate some 6,500 people, and at times did so, including some 500 more or less permanent residents who had been bombed out of their homes. The arches had been largely whitened and fitted out with electricity and efforts were made to improve ventilation but brick built blast walls were also erected at various points. The office staff had their own shelter which was equipped with telephones intended to enable them to carry on working during raids. Although the Headquarters of the railway had been evacuated to Deepdene near Dorking, a room full of telephones was set aside for them should the invading jackboot have trampled through leafy Surrey. Having been hit by 66 bombs Waterloo emerged from the War, scarred as so many stations were but not as badly as some other SR stations. Nevertheless in a very symbolic gesture the glass panels for the roof were replaced in 1946. Despite the shortage of rolling stock and traction power with what remained having been the victim of excessive working and reduced maintenance schedules at Waterloo the railway faced a demand for increased holidays as well as playing its part in the return of de-mobbed servicemen. On summer Saturdays the concourse and surrounding streets were often filled to overflowing which meant there was an excuse to pull the Pullman cars, stored during the war, back into service on the newly introduced "Devon Belle" in 1947.

War-time scars were still evident when the centenary of a station loosely on that site took place on 11th July 1948. For the centenary the famous Mackie painting was produced, and as part of the celebrations on the first day an old Adams express engine (no. 563) and a tricomposite coach in their original liveries were brought to the station, that huge edifice which had grown from such humble

Joseph Locke (1805 – 1860) was Engineer of the London & Southampton when Watlerloo was planned.

beginnings. A daily census for the centennial year also shewed the huge increase in traffic: 1,185 trains in 24 hours (132 arriving between 7 and 10a.m. and 137 leaving between 4 and 7pm). Within the whole railway ensemble with "Waterloo" in the station name there were the 21 platforms in Waterloo, four in the former Waterloo Junction and six underground platforms covering three tube lines.

In 1948, in what was a return to the architectural vandalism of the 1864 bridge, the cab yard roof opposite the section of offices with Platforms 12 to 15 behind them, was extended by 135' largely for the benefit of the boat train traffic. Slightly more harmoniously the Southern Railway installed much smaller plaques to commemorate their dead than the L&SWR and only generically commemorated the number who died in Hitler's war. It is not clear if this was shortage of space or not but the plaques remain to this day, reinforcing the Victory Arch if not the hope of peace that it also represented.

However the decision to hold the Festival of Britain in 1951 also benefitted the railway station, boosted its fortunes, and ensured some renovations.

CHAPTER EIGHT

British Rail and decline

The extensive Luftwaffe bomb damage in the area around Waterloo was a big influence in its selection as a site for the Festival of Britain. The bomb clearance, and the bomb damage to other buildings meant a wholesale clearance was necessary and it was also to be the end for the Lion Brewery, that earlier perceived obstruction to the L&SWR. Demolished in 1950 one of the iconic lions was placed at the York Road entrance to Waterloo Station. Evidently Waterloo would play a key part in the travel arrangements for many and the new railway management accordingly made arrangements.

Two key areas for action in this regard were the erection of the York Road footbridge and another was to widen the Station Approach. However, mundane day-to-day life continued with the approval for the use of an ice-cream fridge in the cinema being granted on 26th February 1950.

The LCC agreed provision of the footbridge, for which part of the brick wall of Waterloo was to be temporarily removed, was their financial responsibility but work would be executed from Waterloo. Costs were estimated at £17,050 (£14,500 for the bridge, contingencies at 10% (£1,450, supervision at 5% of the sum plus a further 10% contingencies became £800 = £16,750 and charges for storing and handling at £300). BR Suggested the LCC should pay for lighting separately.

Whilst accepting the cost of maintenance and lighting on the York Road footbridge the LCC quibbled, on 26th October, about paying for lighting on the Hungerford Bridge extension. This dispute about the Hungerford Bridge extension in no way marred the working relationships about the York Road footbridge where agreements

Abba won the 1974 Eurovision Song Contest wlth the song "Waterloo", promtping this publicity shot.

about encroachments on property were held to be possible solely by correspondence.

Waterloo Station authorities however took a more robust view about the desire of the Festival authorities to have a Festival office. The Festival Office, to be located at the corner of York Road and the exit from the station, was the site of the, now cleared, hitherto bombed out L&SWR former General Offices – the railways wanted a legal contract for such a valuable site. The temporary bridge was also built on the former General Office building site dissecting it approximately into two equal halves some 14' wide between the centres of the trusses.

Widening of the approach road was perhaps a longer-term benefit to Waterloo Station arising from the Festival of Britain.

The 1950s was the final flowering of the Trans-Atlantic ocean-liner and the glamour that was inherent on that form of travel which was soon to be eclipsed by "the jet-set" and mass tourism rather than travel. The ocean-liner expresses started to acquire names such "Cunarder" or "Springbok" or "Statesman" where those trains included First-Class or Pullman carriages of which latter the British Transport Commission took a controlling interest in the Pullman Car Company Limited in 1954, although the company remained a public company responsible to its preference shareholders.

Equally ocean-liner expresses could be named for just the liner itself as when, in early 1957, the "Normandy Express" to Le Havre qualified by including the Pullman car "Myrtle" – the sole survivor of the "Southern Belle" of 1908. Irrespective of nomenclature boat trains usually left from, and arrived, at Platform 11 thereby facilitating the handling of passenger luggage where steamer trunks and other exotic paraphernalia of ocean journeys were easily unloaded from the train into a compound between the platform and the central road for taxis. Not that all was glamour on Platform 11 which also served as the departure point for the 9a.m. to Plymouth a train where the front coach had long been reserved for convicts bound for Dartmoor Prison. (In the Schlesinger film "Terminus" these can be seen being escorted into carriages labelled with delightful euphemism but total accuracy "Home Office Party"!)

Named trains were not confined to expresses for the boat trains. Although the non-stop "Bournemouth Limited" was not reintroduced it was replaced, in 1951, with the "Royal Wessex" and the new BR Mark 1 carriages. This was a period that saw, on summer Saturdays, 19 main-line trains time-tabled to leave Waterloo, but also the era that saw a decline inter alia in specially chartered National Sunday League agency trips, as well as a reduction in day-trips to see ocean-liner arrivals at Southampton. All was not gloom however the era also saw a continuation of well-filled passenger trains to Bournemouth and Portsmouth, as well as a rise in "Ramblers

Specials" which latter continued until ramblers decided it was more environmentally friendly to travel by car.

Waterloo was at the first wave of electrification but even then, and perhaps because of that, as well as the fact Southern Railway was created from different companies who had pursued different approaches, there was a need to consider electricity modernisation. At Waterloo alone there were four different supplies – a 440 volt 3 phase @25 cycles a second; 250 volts DC (came from the preceding supply after some rectification); 660v DC Traction conductor rail system,; and the London Electricity Board supplied various shops in particular at 415 volts, 3 phase at 50 cycles a second. Authorised by Railway Executive Minute 6020/48 of 12th July 1951 rationalisation became a live issue for discussion within BR.

Of more immediate impact to the station was that, by September 1951, discussions were in place to remove the bridge erected for the Festival of Britain and to seek to place a glazed light in the north wall of the Rotunda with gardens on the site of the Old Office building. Of eight companies approached to dismantle the bridge four declined (including Costains!) and four tendered. The lowest price tendered, on 1st April 1952, was £4,576/6/2 from Demolition & Construction Co Ltd who wanted 16 weeks to complete the works. The tender was recommended for acceptance on 19th June 1952 the total cost to the Railway Executive being £10 for the dismantling of the gate in the Rotunda Archway.

For those intrigued about the legend that became the BR Sandwich the London School of Hygiene and Tropical Medicine study group spills the beans admirably. In the "sandwich preparation depot beneath one of the Waterloo cafeterias" Waterloo was the hub for all sandwiches across the main London termini of BR, as well as the packed meals for restaurant cars from Waterloo. The basement unit for the BR sandwich, although how it dared call itself by such a name was a mystery it being more "the sandwich that dare not speak its name", produced up to 4,000 dozen rounds a day in summertime! Barely fit for human consumption there was little humanity in the manufacture of the legendary "sandwich" with bread and rolls cut and

A pair of British Rail Class 423 electrical multiple units at Waterloo in 2003. (Phil Scott)

buttered by machinery; the fillings were also "lovingly prepared" in a similar manner. Humour aside the sandwich production was profitable and it was interesting that it was centred on Waterloo, the terminus with generous arch provision and, unlike St Pancras for example with vaults storing Midland beer, no heavy freight purpose.

Despite road widening works in Approach Road it was still not good enough! The cab drivers raised concerns with members of The London and Home Counties Traffic Advisory Committee. The cabbies were dissatisfied with the exit onto York Road from the station, meaning a member of the London and Home Counties Traffic Advisory Committee raised concerns with the Ministry of Transport. The Ministry view was that the abutment of the railway bridge restricted visibility over York Road and the short distance between Tenison Way and the exit gates made joining York Road challenging. A meeting between the Metropolitan Police, Ministry, Lambeth Borough Council, and the railway on 16th October 1953 produced an agreement that there was no solution by altering vehicular movements within the station roadways and the only agreed solution was a minor realignment of the road to the south at the exit point. The British Transport Police, however, did not like the road widening proposal (it would have meant removing the Festival of Britain Booking Office which was being converted into their offices) as well as citing other safety concerns.

Against a background of some 250,000 people and some 1,500 trains a day using Waterloo, increasing strain on the electricity supplies were a real challenge. A Southern Area Board memo of 22nd November 1956 about the rationalisation of Waterloo electricity supplies, outlined the provision of an 11kv 50 cycle supply from a new 3000 kVa, 33/11 kv transformer and, with the expected rationalisation of suppliers and a desire for improved lighting, two additional transformer sub-stations with 2x 1000 kVa -11000/415v transformers. Further equipment was needed to update the substations at Waterloo and the Waterloo and City – which latter was felt to be satisfactorily dealt with by feeding it power from the Milk Arch sub-station rather than the two main substations needed for the change of electric frequency scheme. The two new transformer substations were to be located one each at Mepham Street and the Milk Arch thereby doubling the number in each location.

Whilst consideration of electricity was underway, it was perhaps ironic that, on 7th March 1957, the RAF decided to name an engine after Biggin Hill - not surprisingly choosing one of the "Battle of Britain Class" steam locomotives. Perhaps more concerning was that only the RAF could send their officers in best "Keith Park" white overalls for a ride on the footplate of a steam engine!

The ironies around power were further compounded when, in 1958, BR cited their heaviest train ex Waterloo as being the steam-drawn 1.15 a.m. West Country newspaper train. Pre-War this train had not appeared in the schedules but war-time exigencies meant it had been used to convey servicemen and the genie was well out of the lamp so BR accepted reality and the train appeared in the public schedule. According to BR this train was a 450-ton configuration which served 95 stations and comprised 15 vehicles on Tuesdays to Fridays, extended to a staggering 17 carriages on a Monday morning when weekend revellers were returning to barracks or homes and which could mean trains were longer than the platforms.

Operationally the Dorchester and Weymouth mail was almost as much of a problem since it required the use of two platforms. Scheduled to leave from Platform 10 at 10.35 p.m. the Dorchester and Weymouth mail train was run up from Clapham Yard with parcel vans and passenger carriages in Platform 10 and the Travelling Post Office with the mail vans loaded at Platform 11. The obligation to carry parcel freight generally reduced capacity for suburban commuter services in the evening because freight stock occupied Platforms 12 and 15 also being loaded at a time when peak passengers wished to travel, however the chaos was nowhere near that which had prevailed in the earlier station ensemble.

The strain caused by freight operations, and whatever the weight of gargantuan trains, the actual number of trains going into Waterloo was a varied picture in 1958. Off-peak trains serving suburbia were reduced from three to two an hour in 1958, which atypically reduced the number of scheduled trains in the station. However Waterloo usage was variable still because of the ocean-liners –in August 1958 94 Specials were run, and on 28th August alone nine left Waterloo between 7.05 and 10.35 a.m. still accommodating the regular traffic.

After the Festival of Britain road and bridge works were completed, it was around May/June 1959 that the Ministry of Transport seemed to discover the existence of the fund set up under the 1899 Act! The Ministry took the view it was for the LCC and Lambeth to determine how the fund should be applied in the Terms of the Act. It was felt that a retrospective application to the Fund for the Festival of Britain works was now a little late and the file was held open should there be major works in the immediate vicinity of Waterloo – which was what the L&SWR had set it up for (S8 part 3). This was a classic case of the LCC applying for Ministry grants when they held funds they could spend on highway works, with the approval of the Lambeth Council. Given that the fund was £30,000 and by July 1957 was at a book value of £185,000 this is quite some lapse!

The global ocean travel sector declining meant rationalisation of rail services was as inevitable as it was predictable. The spectre of the old enmity the L&SWR had had towards the GWR must have been assuaged when, as liners became less attractive to those passengers enraptured by air-travel, boat trains from Paddington to Weymouth were transferred to the rival Waterloo-Weymouth routes from 3rd November 1959.

The principles underpinning the extraordinary desire to build an aerodrome on the roof of Waterloo were revisited in the late 1950s with some staff at Waterloo openly "looking forward" to it in 1956. The Committee on Planning of Helicopter Stations in the London Area was made up of very many representatives from the Ministry of Aviation and several from the London County Council, British Transport Commission, and British European Airways. Whilst it should be remembered that helicopters were seen as the "go-ahead" way of travel it still seems perplexing that the Civil Service seemed to have learnt nothing from the aerodrome idea. A BTC report of 30th March 1960 reported:-

"It is difficult to see how this site could be developed with a helicopter platform over the station without, perhaps, contemplating the re-design and re-building of much of the station with all that would involve in traffic interruption.

Problems would arise in providing space at station level for a ramp and/or lifts to the helicopter platform, and the exclusion of daylight from the station and railway offices would cause serious difficulty. There is already a scheme for office development under consideration"

The 20th meeting of the Committee met on 14th April 1960 and pending some details on Charing Cross it was decided to narrow the study to Cannon Street Station, St Katharine Docks and two sites at Nine Elms, either the Goods Yard or an extended riverside site. The report as submitted commented on the reasons for rejecting Waterloo;-

"The station roof offers an area of about 11 acres. A platform would have to be at least 73ft. above the level of the station concourse if railway activity was not to be interfered with. The practical problems of building a suitable platform are extreme and even then there would be a shortage of space to house terminal facilities. Although the site has excellent access to the West End by road and public transport, for safety reasons it could not be used by single-engined helicopters. The surrounding area contains two large hospitals, a number of large offices, residential areas and the Festival Hall, and multi-engined helicopters could not avoid passing over these while at low-heights."

The Second Draft of the Report had concluded, "Waterloo Station, though ideal from an access point of view, would give rise to serious nuisance through noise and would be excessively costly to build....while Waterloo, lacking river approaches, would be closed to single-engined operations. There would be difficulty....accommodating car parking and ancillary facilities".

Interestingly the Report commented that 4,000 people lived within a quarter of a mile radius and 17,000 within a half-mile radius of Waterloo, but seemed to have no view how they would welcome the concept. The idea of an helicopter platform above the station was even more bizarre when considering how busy the station itself was. BR Southern Region proclaimed Waterloo its busiest station, handling 1,238 trains, and 194,063 passengers every weekday and nearly 600,000 seat reservations a year. Whilst the area of the station remained static at 24 ½ acres, and platforms still numbered 21 (the running roads were 31), all platforms were by now longer than the platform roof line with the total length of platforms promoted as 14,628' - No 11 being the longest at 946'. Even BR admitted, "At peak times the station is working to full capacity – and the number of passengers continues to grow" commenting that in 1939 the daily passenger figure was 156,497 and that since then the number in the busiest single hour of the peak had nearly doubled from 25,929 to 46,697. The situation was not always easier on a weekend, BR citing that, on a busy Saturday in summer, 119 main-line trains left the station carrying 45,386 holidaymakers. This busy traffic was still handled by the power-operated 1936 signal box; at this stage the box was described as having 148 track circuits, 12 train describers, and 309 miniature levers.

Despite the mighty performance of the signal box a rare but serious accident happened on 11th April 1961. During the evening peak,

In 1903 politician Joe Chamberlain had a tumultuous welcome at Waterloo returning from his trip to South Africa.

around 5.20, an electric train passed a signal clearly set at "danger" and, some 400 yards outside Waterloo, collided with Crewkerne, the Bulleid Pacific, legitimately crossing several tracks on its way back to the Nine Elms Depot. The driver of the electric train was crushed and killed in his cab. However whilst railway accidents involving trains at Waterloo are quite rare, at this period the number of staff fatalities averaged around 40 a year.

Pedestrians crossing safely to use the terminus were also a matter of some concern. On 20th May 1961 the LCC asked for a Report from Scott & Wilson, Kirkpatrick & Partners Consulting Civil and Structural Engineers of 47 Victoria Street SW1 on the "feasibility of providing permanent access from the concourse of Waterloo Station to the East Side of York Road. Arrangements had already been made by the LCC and others for access to be provided within the Waterloo Development Building to the East Side of York Road on the site of the former L&SWR General Office Buildings. Later to be known as Elizabeth House, the office building was developed by John Poulson, who would achieve notoriety for his extensive generosity to a range of contacts including some in BR Southern Region. As a result of building Elizabeth House it would be necessary to move the Lion that had formerly graced the Lion Brewery and in 1965 it was moved yet again, even further away, at Westminster Bridge.

The bridge proposals consisted of a post-tensioned concrete deck surfaced with ceramic tiles of the same type as those used on the York Road footbridge and within the Waterloo Development Building enclosed by precast concrete louvres supporting a roof consisting of precast concrete edge and transverse beams covered with wood wool slabs and bituminous felt waterproofing to protect pedestrians from inclement weather. The bridge was to be supported on the Waterloo Development Building at one end and on a column, supported by a pile cap founded on cast-in situ and bored concrete piles, within the Post Office Yard. Providing a support on or immediately adjacent to Waterloo Station with a single span across the Post Office Yard was preferred by both the British Railways Board and the Post Office. However, due to the Waterloo and City Line tunnels and other factors, a single span was economically unfeasible so both the British Railways Board and the Post Office agreed to the provision of a column within the Post Office Yard. It was considered that an experienced contractor should have no difficulty in completing the construction of the bridge within a period of six months for an estimated cost of approximately £20,000.

The design was prepared in conjunction with LCC and Shell Architects and, within the LCC, Sir Hubert Bennett was personally involved in the design. With part of the footbridge approach from Shell Building already constructed and paid for by Shell, the general appearance of the rest of the bridge, for which LCC claimed a grant from the Government of £22,000, was to some extent constrained although the Civil Servants felt able to question the fixing of the 2" thick marble slabs on the fascia.

By 3rd October 1961 the LCC were advised the bridge was planned as a continuous reinforced concrete structure of two spans of approximately 79' and 37' supported on the York Road wing of the Shell Centre at one end, the proposed Waterloo Development at the other and the pier was to be located in the footpath on the West footpath of York Road. The bridge was, in accordance with LCC requirements to be surfaced with precast reconstructed stone paving flags of the same type as would be used on the continuation of this bridge within the Shell centre, and railings of the same design as those being used on the continuation of the bridge within those offices. With atypical local authority parsimony it was recommended that "the most economical, simplest, and aesthetically pleasing method of lighting on this bridge will be to rely on the existing street lighting which could be augmented if necessary". However the cost estimates had increased to approximately £25,000.

In the interim, whilst the discussions about bridges went on, there was still the matter of crossing York Road at street level. The very first Panda Crossing was opened outside Waterloo Station on 2nd April 1962, although it vanished just five years later, along with the other 39 in the country, thereby showing less resilience than the endangered but real pandas. Seen as an upgrade to the conventional zebra crossing, and designed to speed traffic flows in increasingly congested streets, this experiment was opened on York Road some 10 yards to the south of where the main pedestrian crossing is today. The location was selected because it formed a "desire line" outside the then tube station entrance, before that was demolished and replaced, with the modern Shell Building entrance on the opposite side of the road.

Within the station itself catering facilities were now generally operated by British Transport Hotels Limited (BTH). At this busy station catering was supplied from six convenient points, augmented by a concourse trolley service on occasion. The Tea Bar was under the cinema (at Platform 1), an Auto-buffet by the entrance to Platform 9; Surrey Room , above the Enquiry Office Block ; the Horseshoe Bar adjacent to the Enquiry Office; the Long Bar, behind the Windsor Line booking Office, and the Windsor Tea Room – opposite the escalators between Platforms 15 and 16.

Naturally this conveniently spaced catering provision met the beady eye of the "rationalisers" and "modernisers". In a letter of 11th January 1963 E.K. Portman-Dixon, the delightfully titled "Chief of Restaurant Cars and Refreshment Rooms" complained, "we seem to be back to the drawing board", and stated that merging all the facilities together was not likely to be commercially viable. Some within BR were concerned that venues such as the Surrey Room (and the Chatham Room at Victoria) had around 40% of the running costs made up of wages leading, they claimed, to low profitability and low returns (on limited opening hours!).

Undeterred, on 17th January, the proposals from the princes of catering seemed to be "the concentration of our services on concourse level with the Horseshoe Bar going right through to the far end of the present Main Line Booking Hall. The region would probably develop office accommodation above.

As an interim measure because this scheme is likely to take some years to develop, it was agreed that, with the minimum structural work, we should proceed with our proposals for the Windsor Tea Room and the Long Bar

We would then be able to close the Surrey Room, reorganise our services so as to be able to supply the Windsor tea room kitchen, and I shall look into the probability of being able to close down the Restaurant kitchen entirely"

Proposals to relocate the Windsor Line ticket Office were welcomed by BTH on 2nd April 1963 "from a commercial aspect this would be most valuable to me in the presentation of our premises which are, at the present time, so badly obscured"

LSWR Class T9 4-4-0 No.30702 photographed in June 1959. The class was in service from 1899 to 1963.

As the catering saga began so the footbridge decision making saga concluded. On 16th July 1963 the Ministry of Transport Highways Engineering, Bridges Branch advised:- Mr H.C. Adams has examined the drawings for the footbridge and has decided that it will not be necessary to submit the design to the Royal Fine Arts Commission" which, in light of the longevity of the bridge, may perhaps have been a mistake!

Matters were clearly no swifter in catering because, on 24th Feb 1964, Portman-Dixon wrote, "...a scheme has been prepared for converting the Windsor Tea Room to a high class catering establishment giving service throughout the day from breakfast time to supper time, also a lounge bar, all at an estimated cost of £25,000. As a result of this conversion we would be able to close the Surrey Room including the kitchen and Still Room, with most substantial economies, yet maintaining a good and more varied service. This work would comprise Stage 1 of the Waterloo rationalisation.

Stage 2 would involve the reorganisation of the Long Bar. When both stages are completed the net minimum financial improvement anticipated would be £25,000 per annum….."

Licensing Justices cleared the catering scheme by 31st March 1964 and, separately, Portman-Dixon was notified the Southern Area Board was the appropriate level of authorisation for these works on 19th March – being advised the Board next met on 2nd April followed by 7th May 1964

The "Rationalisation and modernisation of catering facilities" memo of 10th April 1964, iterated the Windsor Room conversion costs of £25,000. Involving additional net outlay of £21,000, gains amounting an additional minimum of £37,000 extra on net revenue (before charging interest) which were calculated based on salary savings of £19,287 and assuming £17,978 increased receipts. The balance of expenditure for the wanton barbarism was British Transport Hotels £9,620, and BR £15,380. With the Eldorado of 148% improvement on net revenue against capital outlay the seeds of change, built on a chimera, were set. The inevitable research team had been set up to look at passenger flows and they had established that the Long Bar and the Windsor Room were adjacent to the "centre of gravity" for pedestrian movement. This catering scheme proposed that, between May and August 1964, the Windsor Rooms be divided with 1/3rd becoming the Windsor Bar, and 2/3 "The Thames" which was to be "a high class establishment giving a service of breakfasts, morning coffee, lunch, teas, and suppers". Stage 2 of the proposals was to be the "modernisation" of the Long Bar and, separately at a future stage the proposals for handing the Surrey Room over for staff facilities would be worked on.

Authority was given for Phase 1 on 7th May 1964 by D.V. Ellison Works and Planning Manager for O. McKenna the General Manager at British Railways Southern Region. Authorisation from BTH followed on 14th May.

In June/July 1964, it was very hot, leading to an exchange of memos about poor ventilation in the Long Bar in the evening. While the works were reported to be in hand the inevitable bureaucratic blame-game had to comment "The situation was not improved when the Booking Office was built in front of our windows but this was before we had any control, i.e. in the old Southern Railway days."

Meanwhile, back on the railway the Atlantic Coast Express finally departed Waterloo in September 1964 when the working of all lines west of Salisbury was transferred to BR Western region. The departure of the Atlantic Coast Express allowed the introduction of a Waterloo-Exeter "semi-fast" hauled by the relatively rare sight at Waterloo Station of main-line diesels, of the Warship class.

If the Atlantic Express had gone, the rows about catering had not gone away and on 20th January 1965 Portman-Dixon complained he had just been made aware "there is now a major face-lift proposed for Waterloo and the idea may be revived of putting the main ticket office in the Long Bar area in which case of course there would be a reversion especially to the outline plan prepared some years ago when we were to have a main catering block adjacent to and including the present Horseshoe Bar. Not surprisingly Portman-Dixon thought he would have to put his works on hold and continued to express his concern - "Region keep altering their minds". Clearly, however, Region had access to the same data about the gravitational attraction of this part of the station – BTH could hardly be surprised that the core business would want to utilise that high-demand area.

During the abstract discussions and inter-departmental warfare about station catering came the opening of the bridge connecting Waterloo to the South Bank complex. The noble and lofty ideals, perhaps marred by typical State Brutalism of architecture, of a cultural complex on London's South Bank on the former Festival of Britain site, whatever the (lack of) architectural merits, naturally needed Waterloo to play its part. Culture in grey concrete slabs along the banks of the river flowing through the nation's Capital is not quite as the French would have done it perhaps? The first visible link between the by now nationalised Waterloo Station and the state sponsored arts sector, the high-level walkway was very much in the idiom of council flat "walkways in the skies". Emerging from the Windsor Line/Khartoum end of the Waterloo concourse on 11th October 1965, the walkway may not have been very attractive but there was a feeling of safety for suburban-ites venturing into the "sink of depravity" that is the "edgy metropolis" and gave wonderful connections to Charing Cross, Hungerford Bridge and the South Bank walkways. Given the roads around the Station the bridge was also very practical – and a source of wonderment for a small boy to be able to see so much!

Within BR the warring barons were again trying to establish ascendency at Waterloo. Fuelled by early sixties affluence, already beginning to wane, and the general "go-ahead" ethos it was decided that a station completed barely forty-three years earlier needed a major face-lift and so the barons all met in a Working Party. At the second meeting of the Waterloo Major Face-lift Working Party, on 17th June 1965, it was confirmed that all plans were under active review. Significantly greater weight was attached to the main location of the booking office at this juncture although in July 1965 it was confirmed that the idea of shopping centres in London termini was still "live" but that as Liverpool Street was the priority Waterloo and Victoria were waiting on developments. It did not help Waterloo's retail cause that there was not even universal agreement on whether retail units should be located in a central spine down the centre of the concourse, or scattered to the edges.

The BRB Chief Medical Officer opined that a Medical Centre should be retained on 18th April 1966. This was perhaps understandable since Waterloo was the only London terminus with such provision to itself – Kings Cross and St Pancras having a shared facility – and had had such for some 18 years. Whilst Necropolis may have been largely gone the Waterloo Medical Facility now handled an average of ten people a year brought into the medical centre dead.

A dose of reality was injected when the Chief Accountant of the BRB commented on the facelift proposals. Writing on 19th April 1966 the Accountant drew attention to the fact he had not been included in the notional figures computation, dryly remarking of the "prestige toilet accommodation" that "it would appear the estimated additional annual receipts are not significant enough to be mentioned specifically". Equally, on the same day, Portman-Dixon, now less exotically styled the General Manager at British Rail Catering, sent a memo that the costs of the works to alter the Long Bar/Horseshoe Bar/Windsor Room/Surrey Room cited at £75,000 he felt to be too low, and that the £50,000 net betterment in the figures was likely to be nearer £30,000. Even allowing for the well-worn public-sector "economics" where costs are reduced (to be recouped later once the works are committed and underway as "unforeseen overruns") and benefits inflated (to be explained away later by "failure to implement the plans as predicted) these were serious challenges to the plans demonstrating a lack of rigorous testing.

As if queries about the costs were not enough two days later, on 21st April 1966, the Chief Operating Officer of the BRB could only "support in general terms" the Southern Region face-lift proposals. Amongst other queries serious concerns were expressed about the provisions within the ocean-liner terminal as well as indicating uncertainty about recompense from the shipping companies. Concern was also expressed about the barrier screen's necessity with the "likely" ticket inspection and collection being on train.

By June 1967 the phasing out of steam was under way and would be completed by spring 1968.

Three days later, 24th April 1966, the Chief Commercial Manager felt the need to memo his concerns about the proposed station face-lift. The Chief Commercial Manager's concerns included the obstruction to passengers that may come from the central tenancy spine, and questioning the use of the new flooring materials "over an area as large as the Waterloo concourse". Other concerns included a wish to see the departure times at each barrier not just the destination and in a glorious nod to past nomenclature within Waterloo, "especially in view of the considerable traffic to Clapham Junction for Central Section services" ; querying the cost of the prestige toilet and wanting the new ticket office open in time "for the new electrified service if at all possible".

By the 18th May Portman-Dixon was contributing his feeling that, within the wider proposals for Waterloo, automatic vending should be considered, "in view of the labour difficulty and the long hours of service necessary" but retaining the ability "deal with the more substantial and better class requirements by the new sprig service method". Alcohol vending, Portman-Dixon considered, could be met by "a good popular bar, a bar to draw off the railway staff element and the less desirable bar frequenters, and a compact but attractive bar for the better class passengers".

Despite the seeming lack of harmony among all the Chiefs proposals for changes to Waterloo went to the British Rail Board's (BRB) Planning Committee in June 1966. Approval to develop proposals for Waterloo Station was given, there being a recognition Waterloo remained the most prestigious "showcase" within Southern Region.

Confidence was not full in the schemes despite the BRB approval since the economy was uncertain. Portman-Dixon wrote to McKenna, the General Manager at Waterloo, that he had gathered from a meeting of the BTH Board "that substantial schemes projected....cannot be proceeded with and that we are likely to have an austerity programme for some considerable time to come" and wondering if he could just "at a moderate cost convert the outmoded Windsor Tea Room" akin to "The Ridings" at Kings Cross. Portman-Dixon maintained his new scheme for the Windsor Tea Room would enable BTH's seeming idée fixe against the Surrey Room, which he rather bizarrely felt "is so located as to have no chance of doing all-day business" to be closed, and "the better class travellers commuting from Waterloo" would have a new facility.

McKenna replied to Portman-Dixon on 16th September 1966 apologising for the delay "but I have been waiting to see which way the winds of crisis were blowing". McKenna assured "while the scheme may be slightly delayed at the start we are going ahead with all the work originally planned" and expressing the view the Windsor Tea Room "cannot continue in business beyond 18 to 24 months".

On 17th November 1966 it was anticipated agreement would be secured to incur £4,250 on shop-fitting works to the Windsor Room to be undertaken by Messrs Edmonds. Agreement for works to the Windsor Room was confirmed on 23rd November – the rush being to catch the Christmas trading. The Windsor Tea Room was, somewhat unimaginatively, renamed "The Windsor" to reflect the new trendy status.

Despite the limited funds for the initial station face-lift proposals it was still clear, in March 1967, that the train operating division wanted the Long Bar/Windsor Tea Room which Portman-Dixon wanted. It was equally clear that Portman-Dixon wanted rid of the Surrey Room which was not covetously sought by anyone else! On the 9th March Portman-Dixon relayed a scheme whereby the Surrey Room would contain part of the mess for those at the Charing Cross Hotel and the General Manager's mess at Waterloo, while the rest would be occupied for "certain staff amenities for Officers and the like required by us".

By 17th April 1967 enthusiasm was waning for a "central spine" indeed "Since the meeting of the Working Party held on 30th November last, the Waterloo Face Lift has not made much progress" At this point WH Smith were thought to be the only ones suitable for the centre retail spine

The seemingly perennial obsession amongst the BR team at Waterloo about the social standing of taxpayers that used their station continued when on 19th April R.V. Acres, Public Relations and Publicity Office, wrote that removing the Auto Food Bar was desirable "because, as you know, this causes great trouble late at night in attracting undesirable characters". Portman-Dixon responded on 28th April 1967 supporting retention of the auto buffet and the concourse trolleys which provide "a very substantial amount of money at a high rate of profitability". Not unreasonably Portman-Dixon pointed out "For the year 1966 the auto buffet gross receipts were £27, 411 with a working surplus of 21.6%. The gross receipts for the trolleys were £94, 450 with the very high working surplus of 24%".

As summarised in a Memo of 14th June 1967, from the Administration (Planning) Section of the General Manager's Office, and augmented by related correspondence, the Waterloo proposals were wide ranging:-

The elimination of GPO parcels traffic from the station (thereby allowing the location of a new passenger terminal building for ocean-liner traffic on Platform 11)

The Medical Centre relocated so it was adjoining the Post Office, in the existing Baggage Office position.

The master-plan continued with proposals to replace all four

The West Country Class, here at Waterloo, entered service in 1945 to haul passenger and freight traffic.

existing refreshment rooms with a single catering block, at concourse level, from the Cab Road Arch to the then Baggage Hall. This would replace the Horseshoe Bar, Ladies' Toilets, information office, main ticket hall. The less than aspirational catering aim was "a restaurant of reasonably high standard…The Surrey Room will be closed, and catering of this type will no longer be provided at Waterloo." The Surrey Room was considered for Catering Offices and mess facilities.

Replacing the refreshment trolleys with "small permanent catering buildings, integrated with other tenancies"

A new "combined ticket and enquiry office" was to be located at the site of the Windsor Room, Long Bar and Till Called For (TCF) office. A smaller ticket office, however, only selling main line tickets for Woking and beyond, would be located where the taxis arrived, and formed from part of the Baggage Office opposite Platform 5. The Baggage Hall was scheduled for closure.

Locating the TCF to the Colonnades area, connected to the concourse level, by a lift to the Luggage Hall

A wish to put estate tenancies on the central spine, and ensuring they were in uniform units rather than the existing varied ones, all to be connected by a low roof with inbuilt lighting. The idea of connecting the tenancy blocks by such a “roof within a roof” was speedily discounted however. The influence of W.H. Smith and Boots was made clear when the Estates Manager pointed out that interim trading units would be needed since those two stores yielded a net rental income of “some £29,000 per annum”

The twin Gods of Rationalisation and Modernity, were to be further appeased by locating left-luggage and telephone points at more regular intervals along the platform barrier line – itself to be brought 6’ further into the concourse, modernised with automated train indicators and an advertising screen. Current advertising revenues were £33,000 which it was felt could be more than doubled.

Modernised toilet facilities to be “semi-prestige and ordinary standard”! Prestige was to be at the Windsor end, ladies at concourse level and gentleman’s area to take over the Faulkner premises in the existing gentleman’s toilets. The existing toilets at the eastern end of the platform were to be “divided into two portions, to provide non-prestige toilets for both sexes”

Messrs Faulkner’s were to have their tenancies terminated and “a prestige type of hairdressing salon for ladies and gentlemen will be located adjoining the ‘superloos’”

Improved seating (“limited extent”); modernised concourse, including rubber tiles for the concourse, as laid at, of all non-prestigious places, Cannon Street Station; improved concourse and façade lighting, and general decoration upgrading.

Whilst these Reports regularly use “modernisation” and “rationalisation” ad nauseum throughout, almost as touchstones of a “go-ahead” mentality, there is no evidence adumbrated about public dissatisfaction! Indeed the tenancies, which contributed to the “dismal appearance of the station”, were popular enough to yield a net income of £60,000 whereas by incurring extra expenditure of £17,000 BR thought they could achieve another £5,000 a year. As so often this financial projection was to assume that customers would just do as they were expected and not exercise choice, or refuse to like the "improved" offer. All works were, in total, budgeted at £460,000 and throughout the memo the only four proposals that had a justification other than "modernisation" or "rationalisation" were: moving forward the ticket barriers (to create a circulation space between platforms – clearly a staff wage saving proposal); and the lighting, which was indeed still inadequate. Some justification for increased ticket office space was offered; and neither BR nor the GPO were satisfied with parcel facilities which were growing by 20% more than the schedules and it was predicted that by 1968 their current arrangements would be impossible. The other proposals seemed to be "change for change's sake" or, as in the case of the toilets, after a brief nod to "high standards", were solely around profits.

Parallel to discussions about on-platform catering, above platform accommodation was also being enacted! Perhaps even less aesthetic than the "umbrellas" erected by SR' at the end of the platforms was the excrescence erected by BR for trainmen. After steam traction out of Waterloo finished, 9th July 1967, the train crews that used to be based at Nine Elms were brought into Waterloo and housed on an extraordinary construction above the buffer stops near Platforms 1 to 6. The loco-men's construction was of poor design, being wooden and on steel girders, and bore no legibility to the overall design of the platform or concourse towards which it presented a blank face. It can only be hoped it was not as dire for the crews as for those of us who witnessed it although the loco-men got a good view of their passengers – by now some 195,000 a day.

The momentum for the staff to have the Surrey Room really picked up pace in July and August 1967 added to which, by 28th August there was a clear head of steam to take the Long Bar for a Ticket Office, with many memos referring to railway perceptions of unruly elements in the Long Bar. Indeed some staff, if not necessarily all passengers, had welcomed the arrival of The Windsor not only for themselves but for the users of that part of the station and those who desired to escape from the "unruly" elements and on 18th July there was discussion to "retain passenger good will if we could produce a small licensed place on the concourse at the Windsor lines end of the Station".

Against a steadily declining economy the BRB were advised in November 1967 that Waterloo improvement works should be phased: Phase 1 being train information, barriers and advertisements works. The second phase of works would be tenancies, TCF offices, secondary ticket office and the medical centre. The third phase covering the main ticket office, the information office, and catering facilities; concluded by the fourth phase – toilets and lighting. At this point it was mentioned that whilst the announcement system was considered broadly satisfactory it was felt pre-recorded announcements could be introduced, with a reduction in staff keeping enough to cope with exceptions, which was perhaps as well since the expected programme costs for all phases was now £565,000.

Less controversially 1967 saw the addition of a fourth escalator from the Northern Line tube connection to the Waterloo Station, this being welcomed by the far from pithily named: Transport Co-ordinating Council for London Interchanges Group, Waterloo Station Working Party. This "Waterloo Working Party" was concerned that the approach to the station was not sufficiently modern and "go-head" showing signs of Nineteenth Century commerce (bonded warehouses), traces of the Eighteenth Century street patterns, and lots of railway workshops/stores and offices. The Working Party considered therefore Waterloo would benefit from extending the station concourse over Waterloo Road with an escalator/stairway connection to the bus lay-bys sited opposite the undercroft. The existing taxi road was to be pedestrianised and taxis located at a higher level still. Arguably this was the beginning of the modernisation against conservation era for, whilst the L&SWR and their shareholders had been ruthless in building what they needed as "modern" and "go-ahead" a more empowered citizenry were less prepared to take it from a nationalised industry where they felt they were "the shareholders", but within BR the idea was committed for further study.

Where there was a clear evidence of failure was in the passenger experience changing from one form of travel to another. With Waterloo operating on broadly three levels, the station concourse, street level, and subterranean, with different transport of train/bus/tube, the lifts were not adequate to meet demand. As a result a programme was commenced where the lifts began to be replaced with escalators

An additional use for the structure containing the displaced Nine Elms loco-men came in April 1968 when the staff of Thomson Newscaster were located there, projecting in lights a mixture of news and advertisements above the existing cinema. This new service, broadcasting from 4th April, was at least a step to implementation of some coherent action at Waterloo, not otherwise readily evident amongst warring barons of the trading sections!

Within the barons of BR it was clear BTH was very much secondary to King Railway, although how they ever thought they would not be was perhaps a mystery. BTH, who had been complaining the idea had regularly emerged "over the last 20 years" originated a memo, on 4th October 1968, "The Southern Region have now confirmed that they wish us to vacate the Long Bar site during December of this year in order that they can establish the ticket office there".

A memo of October 1968 on the parameters for a popular restaurant made the point that, against a national average of 31% of citizens in A, B, and C1 socio-economic groupings (basically supervisory level and above) Waterloo had 70% users in that category. Two thirds of the station users were male, and they were 2" taller than the national average – all of which data apparently justified the removal of the Surrey Room and Windsor Room with a new "popular restaurant"! The rationale contained language almost out of an Austin Powers movie, with psychobabble that was eminently challengeable, frequently contradictory, and not at all clearly identified with the client group of the day. Apparently "the discreet use of gold in the décor" helped "meet the need to reduce anxiety"; whereas "the need to match the excitement of some customers" could be achieved

The No.602 Squadron locomotive of the Battle of Britain Class. It was in service 1948-67, seen here in 1966.

by "colours towards the warm end of the spectrum", and so on!

Rather more pragmatically a memo of 21st October from Campbell-Smith in catering pointed out the main-line booking area was slightly larger than the Long Bar and that reconstruction of "the Windsor Room" (as the internal memo hybridised the former and current name) could include alcohol vending points and that with four bar serving points and a snack counter that would more than cope with the peak sales of the Windsor Bar, Long Bar, and Surrey Room combined. Such a provision, with The Windsor subdivided into a 1/3 and 2/3 split would cater for the average stop of 9 minutes for alcohol and still allow those who had more leisure. Campbell-Smith had progressed the proposals for alcohol at the Khartoum end by requesting the conversion of a disused waiting room near The Windsor and a 30' x 20' rail bar on the commuter end of the concourse. With detailed plans of the temporary premises promised in a week Campbell-Smith allowing the interior designers a month to draw up proposals with consumer testing in middle of December and a decision around Christmas time.

Duly the consumer research was done on preferred schemes for cutlery, chairs and "offer", with students at the Kingston College of Art undertaking some of the design. As so often this "consultation" was far from perfect since the status quo was not an offer, which effectively undermines the point of true engagement; and the panel was 200 people chosen at random. Wolff Olins who designed an unsuccessful scheme reinforced this point about consultation from a different angle in saying they placed less reliance on consumer feedback because, "...most people are simply incapable of understanding a plan elevation and rendering, and of making a sensible judgement based on it." Thus spake the "go-ahead" tendency – only they are right and citizen agreement is purely for "buy-in" on the terms of the State, ignoring the fact that the citizen is in fact the owner of a nationalised railway system! The BR Design Panel also reflected this elitism: concerned that a popular restaurant at Waterloo should "...accept for the brief the standards set by consumers". It was left to Campbell-Smith to explain the obvious "need in a popular restaurant of this kind to cater for known public demand". Although, in fairness to Michael Wolff it was hard to disagree with his view that "British Rail's attitudes to catering (which I think are unimaginative and reactionary)" were certainly held by many in respect of the famous sandwich.

BTH's gallant rearguard action to keep The Windsor as a cash-cow was again defeated as the train business re-emphasised in January 1969 that they would want the space in approximately 15 months. Campbell-Smith summarised: the process as;-

Create open bar and "quicksnack" at Windsor end: Start May 1969

Vacate Long Bar to allow new Booking Hall: Start August 1969

Create popular restaurant (only drinks with meals) in old Booking Hall: Start December 1969

Close Surrey Room for staff changing rooms etc and close Windsor Restaurant for new reservation office

Create and open lounge bar in the reservation office

If approved "quicksnack" at main-line end

By 25th March 1969 the plans were progressing and it was clear BTH were not in the driving seat by now with greater clarity about timetabling. The fate of the Surrey Room was further justified in a BTH memo of 21st May 1969 which quoted the Shops, Offices and Railway Premises Act of 1963 and mentioned compliance meant changing rooms and staff facilities had to be close to the operations

– hitherto many of these facilities had been at nearby Mepham Street which, whilst nearby, was felt not to meet the statute.

The cinema, by now named "The Classic" had closed in April and the Public Relations and Publicity Committee were informed three months later, on 10th July 1970,

"…that active consideration was being given to the possibility of using the former Classic cinema at Waterloo for screening industrial films generally. It was possible that by charging film sponsors for the use of the theatre at times when it was not required for railway purposes the theatre could be made viable: a licence would be necessary, and the GLC would have to obtain the agreement of the nearest cinema, the National Film Theatre. No difficulty was expected in that respect.

All the seating and projection equipment had been taken away and only the empty shell remained. A party would be visiting the site on 13th July to get an idea of the costs likely to be incurred….."

Perhaps unsurprisingly this idea went nowhere, the idea of a cinema on a piece of expensive London land being a viable commodity "for screening industrial films generally" was one perhaps not envisaged outside the confines of a nationalised industry. A large advertising hoarding soon covered the cinema, the tea room underneath not being affected.

If the lights were going out all over the Waterloo "Classic", the thorough programme to "refurbish, rehabilitate, and modernise" Waterloo began with an illuminating programme of new lighting installation in 1970-1971. All previous lighting had improved the cavernous darkness of Waterloo (and other large stations) but station size had still defeated new technology, and it was time to again bring forth light from the darkness.

Passenger facilities were also overhauled in line with the previous decade's considerations, at the time BR said "modernised" but the paying public were more divided on that point between "modernisation" and "vandalism" at Waterloo. The Long Bar refreshment room, opposite Platforms 13 to 15, became a 16-window ticket office on 6th December 1970 thereby allowing demolition of the Main Line/Main Line Suburban and Windsor Line offices. Whatever the merits of the decision on booking offices, the fact remained that 1971 was a new high for passenger traffic at Waterloo as BR figures at Waterloo showed 55 million passenger trips over the year. Behind the scenes however the British Rail Property Board, working in conjunction with the Region had worked up a proposal for an outline operational brief and engaged consultants to work up the concept. The consultants reported in March 1971, with proposals acceptable to the Region, proposing to demolish everything between the barrier line and Waterloo Road. At a stroke were to go the station buildings, the concourse, the Headquarters Office Buildings and all premises below concourse level! Even on 19th March 1974 BR were saying internally "It is not known when – if at all – such a redevelopment might commence, but further studies are currently in hand.", however this idea never gained sufficient traction.

Back in the reality of "the art of the possible" on 25th January 1972,

the circular buffet opposite Platform 11, which had been trading under the imaginatively named "Horseshoe Bar" became "The Drum", a self-service cafeteria and bar, which "Design" magazine perhaps rather optimistically hailed as marking "the end of the warped sandwich era in British Rail catering and the start of something cleaner, more appetising – and more decorative". The spearhead of a £1 million programme to modernise some 80 BR eating establishments, main contractors for the £61,000 works at Waterloo were David Esdaile Ltd, and the architects for the project were Hulme Chadwick & Partners who added 1,400 sq ft of floor space, by placing the bar on a mezzanine floor. To tie in with the imagery of a "drum" there were cylindrical column casings, downlighters and bar stools and tables to which customers could take segmental trays in "ICE Darvic" – eight of which fit exactly round each table, and for the literal-minded customers there was a drummer boy on the walls.

The taxi rank seen in 1914 with porters and traffic policeman. The taxi rank remains here to this day.

This symphony of drums was made visible from the concourse by two curved windows each of 9' diameter cut from bronze-tinted acrylic sheet cantilevered out over the concourse. The central door pillar and window frames were, thankfully, of the more subdued satin chromed steel.

Humour was not lost within BR however being expressed in a 1972 illustration to show further modernisation proposals. In a set of drawings illustrating works largely realised, we should perhaps be grateful that the boat train was not for the Lusitania as illustrated, and that the adverts for cars did not herald "The New BONZA Range"!

On 12th April 1973 the BR Board discussed a memo, of 6th March 1973, from the Chief Executive (Railways) David Bowick considering how to exploit trading opportunities at stations; a memorandum which placed Waterloo in the second category identified as having been examined and with major opportunities. It was proposed that the delivery mechanism would be to create a Station Trading Division, and the programme would cost around £10,000 000 over five years yielding an annual return of 15%. The Board agreed to go down this road.

Passengers who had wondered why it was necessary to close the ticket offices they used were put out of their misery (of anticipation anyway) in May 1973 when they discovered that the old Booking Hall, the relocation of which had caused the loss of a refreshment room was to be occupied by......a new 119 seat restaurant! Originally named "The Great Express", not something that Waterloo enjoyed a reputation for, unlike the speed-merchants at Kings Cross and Paddington, it was not an unqualified success and later became the "Trafalgar" buffet and bar whilst Trafalgar was Nelson's naval battle not Wellington's land battle at least the marketing men were in the right war! Those commuters expecting they could still enjoy the Surrey Room, which at this stage served 111 meals a day and had scope for more given it was only open from 12 till 3 on 6 days a week, found out however that was to be closed in order to become a staff canteen. The Windsor was also to be closed in accordance with the Master-plan to channel all customers to The Great Express. What

BR seemed not to realise, which, after its initial start at Waterloo Bridge Station, the L&SWR and its successor had, was that Waterloo is an exceptionally long concourse and passengers tend to stay in the vicinity of their departure platform or nearest exit, not be channelled to a centralised service.

If there was vacillation about Waterloo for the citizen commuter the BRB mandarins readily approved, on 10th April 1974, adaptations at Waterloo and Croydon for "Southern Territory Headquarters" at £0.21m.

The "facelift" plan creaked on even though many would have argued the economy was hardly as buoyant as it had been when first thought of some decade before. The B R B Investment Committee met on 4th June 1974 discussing a memorandum of 23rd May 1974 in respect of modernising barriers, advertising, indicators and tenancies,

"Approval is sought to the modernisation of the barrier line at Waterloo Station at an estimated net outlay of £599,000 at 1st quarter 1974 price levels. Within this estimate is a sum of £170,000 for train indicators, and it is proposed to negotiate a single tender with the sole manufacturer"

Hitherto it was stated that minor short-term improvements totalling £620,000 had "been approved at the appropriate level over the last 3 years, and a new travel centre is planned at an estimated cost of £80,000". An infrastructure grant of £240,500 was expected, and after allowing for this it was claimed there would be an improvement on revenue account of £3,000 p.a. and an increase in the social grant of £71,000 p.a. There was no budget provision for 1974 but "there should be no problems in accommodating the required £70,000, which was to be met by cancelling Haslemere station reconstruction. There is, however, inadequate provision in the 1975 programme, a shortfall of £243,000 and assurance is required that the project would have a sufficiently high priority for the shortfall to be provided within the ceiling for London & South East in 1975". This shortfall of £243,000 it was proposed could be met by the £500,000 allocated to unspecified station reconstructions.

A feature of Waterloo for a long time had been the sliding gates at the concourse end of the platforms. These gates were slid across, with varying degrees of compassion and civility, prior to departure and were of the Bostwick variety – the lattice type gates that are pulled across an opening such as a station entrance or lift and named after the company which originally made them. The proposal went on to comment that the existing Bostwick barriers were life-expired, and continued with the opinion that the tenancies along the barrier line were unsightly and allowed users to see debris. Operationally the "present 3 manually operated train indicators are inadequate and confusing", and it was suggested a new control centre, responsible for operating the indicators and announcing equipment would benefit Waterloo if situated with a commanding view over the platforms. It was assumed that if authority for the project was forthcoming by April 1974 on-site works could begin in December of that year with completion in early 1976.

The schemes authorised for Waterloo at regional level in the preceding three years included:-

New ticket office £120,000

Modernisation of concourse lighting £25,000 (the previous lighting indubitably had had the effect of illuminating only the lower half of the concourse)

Remodelling of catering facilities (authorised by British Transport Hotels Ltd) £170,000

At the same time as the Board were considering major investments the work in hand amounted to £177,000 for replacement of escalators to "The Drain" and London Underground; with £128,000 for the improvement of platform lighting. Proposals were also in the ether for a new travel centre, which was to adjoin the new ticket office, for £80,000.

The recommendation was also made to install the Solari indicators paying up to £170,000 to Telesign Ltd whilst the equipment was to be manufactured by Solari of Udine in Italy "who are the only firm capable of producing the type and size of indicators required for Waterloo" but still needed a lead time of 12 months. Executing

The famous clock at Waterloo was installed in 1919 and powered by workings elsewhere in the building.

operation of the Solari sign system was to be conducted from the Waterloo Signal Box. Analysis of pedestrian routes continued to show the focal point of all passenger flows was between Platforms 12 and 15 but since a still significant number did not go there additional large repeater indicators, over the extremities of the concourse, and a small indicator over each platform simply showing the details of the next train from that platform were needed.

The Bostwick barriers, which were stated to be difficult to maintain, were to be replaced, this move having been anticipated by the erection of new ticket collectors' boxes which had been chosen to blend in with the proposed new barriers. To an extent this was not radical, the railways always had their own corporate styles but at least once there had been differences to the travel experience. The dead hand of soul-less corporate design was already descending on the railways and what was trialled in a station at Auchtermuchtie could as easily be put in a great London terminus. Despite this desire for uniformity, a uniformity underscored by the criticism of "…structures of varying age, no common design throughout…" the opportunity was not to be taken to deal with the staff accommodation block surmounting that section of the barrier between Platforms 1 and 6 "…erected some years ago on a line which was then expected to be that of the new barrier". Aestheticism clearly was not the driving force here!

Nevertheless uniformity was the driver behind the barrier line improvements. A uniform barrier line from Platforms 1 to 11 met the uniform barrier line between Platforms 12 and 15 and was linked across the cab road by a high-level advertising display. The new escalator access to "The Drain" then underway, between Platforms 15 and 16, would be roofed over allowing the architectural cohesion to "The Village" (as even BR still called it) accommodation block; the barrier would then continue along the Windsor Line concourse to Platform 21. Because the escalators were under the station roof there was no empiric need to cover over those leading to the Tube, so there is no reason to disbelieve the stated aim of uniformity which some see as indistinguishable from aestheticism. So the barrier works were in many ways an attempt to unify the whole station; whether the work was aesthetic is another matter but that is not to deny the attempt, one rejected by the L&SWR who had supplied a cohesive aesthetic along the wall on the other side of the concourse.

Of course even if the works were aesthetically pleasing mammon may slightly have marred the effect. Approximately 12' above the concourse level the solid screen was to be used for advertising displays between the sites proposed for the three new display indicators. The section above the cab road, opposite the main entrance, as originally conceived, was to be slightly higher and used for advertising of a more "spectacular" style. British Transport Advertising expected to yield an annual revenue increase of £25,600 pa that would yield to the Region an additional £13,056 a year.

The three indicators were a proposal to deal with the perceived problem of the manually operated indicators – one of which was located between Platforms 6 and 7 (displaying main line suburban and main line departures); one between 12 and 13 (principal arrivals); and one between 18 and 19 showing Windsor and Reading line services both arrivals and departures).

BR asserted the arrivals board "...creates much confusion, being located at the busiest part of the station immediately in front of the ticket office" but offered no evidence for this assertion, and then complained "The two departure indicators are remote from this area, and are over 150 yards apart, resulting in considerable unnecessary movement by passengers unfamiliar with the layout or the route system". In fact that was rather the point: the arrivals board at the main entrance was where people greeting passengers would arrive at Waterloo; the departures were separated because nobody travelling to Windsor had the remotest need to know about train departures to Exeter. Having been trialled at Victoria Station the electronic "Solari" signs were selected as the way of advising train arrivals and departures. There were still to be three signs however! The first, and most comprehensive indicator, was to be between Platforms 12 and 15 at the beating passenger heart of the station. 110' long and some 9' high erected some 13' above the concourse this electronic behemoth was to show all departures from the station and a few principal arrivals (four of the 28 columns). Tenancies located over and around the stairs from the concourse to Waterloo Road, near Platform 12 would be removed to the barrier line to aid visibility. Between Platforms 3 and 6 would be a secondary repeater array some 65' long made up of 17 columns. This display was to show all departures from Platforms 1 to 15 inclusive. The Windsor Line maintained its air of semi-detachment from the Waterloo massif by replacing the wooden sign by a Solari repeater in the same spot. Some 30' long and with 7 columns this would show all departures from Platforms 16 to 21. Common to all displays was a clock (two in the case of the main board) under which was kept a space for emergency notices.

Above each platform was a destination departure board, and these were augmented at the foot of each stairway to Platforms 1 to 15 that was accessed from the passenger subway. These signs replaced the venerable fingerboards at passenger gates, supplemented by blackboards giving urgent/emergency information.

Passenger information could be a pressing issue in a station where, BR commented in 1973, that the average daily use of the station was 50% higher than in 1920. BR stated that over 58 million passengers had been carried in 1972 with "The Drain" carrying 10 ¼ million passengers and Waterloo Eastern 9 million.

The 0298 (Beattie Well Tank) class of locomotive entered service in 1863 and ran to the 1960a. (Oxyman)

Station trading, as distinct from "facelifts", was also progressing slowly: the 5th August 1974 Minute of the BR Property Board "suggested that the possibilities in this direction [trading opportunities] should be explored now that the barrier and indicator scheme had been approved". The discussion concluded the work should be done by Healey and Baker or in-house – and that the options were to be explored.

The Project Manager for Station Trading Developments, Bartlett, therefore wrote to his Board on 6th November 1974 stating that Ladbrokes were expressing an interest in being at Waterloo. Ladbrokes were claiming that 83% of their turnover, went back to their customers and that that turnover was of the order of £5-10,000 a week (£260-520,000 a year) depending on the location. Bartlett recommended the idea was given a punt believing BR should be aiming for a 1,000 square foot unit at Waterloo and "should aim to achieve no less than £10,000 minimum from a percentage of net profit."

In November 1974 the Station Trading Report for Waterloo appeared, commissioned internally, with market research of local office workers conducted by Transmark. BR commented unfavourably on shops in the area; those in Lower Marsh dismissed because the "general presentation and standard of Lower Marsh is one of cheapness and lack of quality. The area can be considered similar to Petticoat Lane". York Road retailers may have been pleased to know BR considered, "The presentation and standard of this parade of units is superior to Lower Marsh (although much quieter) and could be likened to a modern New Town development" – which was of little appeal to those of us escaping such a retail offer in our own dreary New Town back-yards! The Cut (an area to the South-east of the station, just off Waterloo Road, which served the local residents) was less judgementally described as being "a parade of shops similar to that in a medium sized town". The Report highlighted the nearest major retail area was across the River at the Strand,

Trading on Waterloo Station was, the 1974 Report continued, yielding in the preceding year, rentals on BR's own shops of £65,000 negotiated with national agreements (this figure excluded the GPO) and a minimum of £17,845 locally negotiated which, with the contribution from Travellers-Fare of £49,771 gave a total of £132,616 generated on the station. The Report also considered Waterloo, with eight concourse entrances/exits and a further nine exits on the platforms, less than ideal, arguing that the passenger arrangements allowed a boycott of a concourse also considered over long and thus impossible to see the whole length (which fact did not preclude Regent Street being a commercial success but what did the Georgians know?) Furthermore the station, "whilst being somewhat more light and airy than some London termini" was felt to still present a "somewhat grimy and unattractive image not helped by the clutter of facilities on the concourse itself".

The Report proposed with only two exceptions, to concentrate all retail offers at the eastern end of the concourse as well as take over some of the ground floor of the office block. It was recognised that the barrier scheme had approval and thought that this would either give the opportunity to dispense with kiosks at the end of platforms and replace them with automated vending machines; or that by adopting the Report proposals and keeping barrier kiosks it would be possible to dispense with all concourse clutter (although at one point the Report raised the idea of a "Victorian market"). The Report commented on retailer resistance to the idea of station trading, and the fact the retail economy was "not expansionary", recognising that it may not be possible to implement all recommendations but that if it was it would cost £563,000 yielding between £167,000 and £249,000 per year.

However on 27th November 1974 a very snippy personal Memo was sent from R.B. Reid General Manager of Southern Region (and future BR Chairman having started as a traffic apprentice at the L&NER) to David Bowick the Chief Exec (Railways) on the BRB. Reid's Memo stated the Report on station trading that had been produced was flawed not having been discussed with him and his team. Reid commented on each proposal such as it "making no sense to put the left luggage facilities down steep flights of stairs" even if the demand for male toilets could be met with only half the facilities. Reid poured scorn on a Tea Bar right across the front of the Great Express restaurant, pointed out the Information Office was still in use and was a Regional plan, that "The Drum's" license depended on the ladies' toilets adjacent being open and that a protuberance in front of that restaurant also made little trading sense. That accommodation was tight for Territorial Headquarters and the Area Manager was accepted in principle if not the detail. On office accommodation shortages Reid, with a delightfully dry wit acknowledged, "Waterloo have already had to despatch the Freight Manager's organisation to Croydon for this reason" but expressed scepticism about the suitability of the former cinema for offices. The proposals for servicing shops from the Station Approach Road were exposed as not recognising the existing road congestion and met the suggestion "Unless this work is confined to the midnight hours, the road congestion under the canopy – which is already almost impossible at times to keep free – would be made that much worse". On the proposal to halve the size of the existing Luggage Hall, Reid commented that the Region were already looking at that in conjunction with their Train Catering Plans; and he concluded "the Report is not a practicable and well-informed approach to the development of retail facilities at Waterloo Station. I suggest the authors are asked to get down to detail, with the help of my Officers, and produce a document which would be worthy of you and your colleagues on the Station Trading Group spending your valuable time in discussing".

Two relatively uncontroversial proposals in the Station Trading Report concerned the cab-way pavement and the Thames Bar. Converting a wide pavement near the cab approach currently used for left luggage lockers and telephone kiosks to a retail area, in Reid's opinion, could be worked on if somewhere else for the cabs waiting for the boat trains could be found. The proposal to convert the Thames Bar into a retail unit (the master plan suggested it itself could be sited in part of the area gained by the creation of the frontage to the Great Express Restaurant) met Reid's masterful nine-word response "This is The Thames Bar at the present time".

Reid forbore to comment in that, in their preamble, the Report authors had made much of the fact that the concourse was long with people using only parts, and that it is impossibile to see from one end to the other – so quite why the authors thought forcing passengers to use toilets at the "wrong end" of the station for them was practical is somewhat amazing!

A proposal of 25th October, in a memo from the Project Manager supporting the approach from operators that amusement arcades be trialled on major stations and particularly while proposals for Waterloo were not finalised, was rejected at a meeting on 29th November 1974. The Board took the view that "this was an emotive issue", which could cause offence and perhaps some commercial backlash, and that Waterloo was not considered a suitable place for an amusement arcade. However, the Board agreed that a discreet experiment with an amusement arcade might be appropriate in the future. A memo, of the same date, from the Chief Officer (Special Duties) to Bowick on the matter of amusement arcades is a gem of

British pragmatic duality. Agreeing that it is an emotive issue and his "Wesleyan Methodist gore rises" the Chief Officer (Special Duties), the redoubtable Michael Bonavia later to be a key player in the Channel Tunnel project and a key writer on railway matters, reminds the Chief Executive (Railways) "but we are professionals and have a statutory responsibility to make money". Continuing in pragmatic vein the memo states "Just think how much the nation profits from human weakness – tobacco, alcohol, gambling, etc. I see no business reason why we should not try for a cut of our own." and, after broadly agreeing the corporate line, concludes "I think a discreet experiment or two would be sensible but I question Waterloo. The population immediately south is a bit raffish: we must avoid accusations that we are encouraging hooliganism."

The same meeting, 29th November 1974, largely sided with Reid and asked the Project Manager to discuss with Southern Region:-

Disadvantages in siting left luggage offices at basement level, and doubts about the gentlemen's facilities being closed.

The acceptability or otherwise of a tea bar across the front of the "Great Express" Restaurant.

Doubts about dispensing with the ladies' waiting room and toilet in view of the licence being granted to "The Drum".

Suitability or otherwise of converting the Cinema to offices.

The encroachment onto the concourse of the automatic revenue collection system.

The ability or otherwise to service shops from the station approach road.

The need to analyse the financial effect of moving facilities from the main concourse, given that WH Smith had already requested a two-storey building to be provided on their existing site.

Whatever the decisions yet to be made the fact remained that BR figures suggested 190,000 people each weekday used Waterloo, of whom 75% were regular commuters – figures that would surely seem unfeasible to W.J. Chaplin when he had been putting Waterloo on the map.

On 15th January 1975 a situation report on the investigation into a

A British Rail Class 458 at Waterloo in 2003. The class of four car units run on the suburban lines. (Phil Scott)

number of stations (Charing Cross, Glasgow Central, Waterloo, Cardiff General) reported that the Waterloo study had been forwarded to Region for consultation purposes on 9th December 1974 "and a date for formal consultation on the proposals contained in it is still awaited."

A report to the Board, of 1st July, from the Station Trading Division, summarised why the Region felt having Waterloo as a major scheme was untenable raising as objections:-

The single storey tea bar extension on to the concourse was "totally unacceptable, because of the intended installation, ultimately, of automatic ticket collection which would itself intrude '18' onto the concourse".

The proposals to close one Ladies' and one Gentlemen's toilet for conversion to other use were rejected on the grounds that "the vast majority of their daily throughput of some 193,000 passengers use non-corridor trains" as well as toilets being used by existing traders, and station staff because there were no public facilities in the immediate vicinity of the station. Toilet closures it was felt could jeopardise renewal of BR Catering Licences. Stunningly, on the longest concourse in the UK, the Trading Division thought one set of toilets at one end of the concourse was enough.

The moving of the left-luggage office, which was to be transferred to the male toilets, despite having an unutilised area was resisted by Region also. Region cited the BRB decision to remove left-luggage lockers which had increased demand at the left-luggage office.

The Luggage Hall proposals were acceptable to Region for trading but while work on the barrier scheme progressed the area would be needed for two years to accommodate displaced tenants and building contractors.

There was no dispute over the former Information kiosk, which had in fact already been offered to WH Smith for occupation once the new Travel Centre was operational.

Proposals for the Cab road pavement were rejected partly because the existing station telephone kiosks had been relocated there but also because of interference with passenger flows.

The existing Area Manager's office was considered expendable if an alternative could be located.

Bartlett, commented in his Memo of 20th October, "With the somewhat increasing tendency for exhibition sites on stations which are controlled by B.T.A. Ltd [British Transport Advertising] to be used for trading activities rather than for pure exhibition purposes [there had been problems from one site user] discussions were held with B.T.A. Ltd with a view to more income being generated from these activities than the fixed site rental arrangements, which B.T.A. Ltd currently operate, allow."

Working on a pilot scheme, with Wallcover Manufacturers Company, exhibition sites controlled by BTA were to be regarded as temporary trading sites "subject to more lucrative percentage rental terms more normal for station trading activities". Operating from 1st October to 31st December 1975 on a number of stations in this trial the trader paid the normal BTA rate plus 2½% of gross turnover. Station Trading Division received one third of the percentage rental turnover.

Originally Waterloo had been intended as the major scheme for station trading but Paddington was substituted in light of obstacles experienced at Waterloo, despite a shortage of information on people and market potential at Paddington. With Waterloo downgraded to a "medium project" "some doubt existed as to whether even this lesser category of development could be maintained" in the words of the Minute, discussions about putting the Area Manager's team into the old cinema continued, as did the idea BR Property Board Staff would move out of their accommodation in the office block

The economy seemed to be tanking on stations across BR and it was noted on 23rd July 1975 that John Menzies were withdrawing from many stations, although most of Menzies units had been subsequently let. Finlay and Co indicated that of their 46 remaining outlets 19 were expected to be economically viable by the end of the year – 14 were uneconomic and the firm wished to close them irrespective of any rental concessions the Board may make, and 13 could survive with concessions. It was considered if Travellers-Fare would take over individual sites if Finlay and Co withdrew. This did not stop "The Drum" being modernised and acquiring a juke box!

The decline in Waterloo's passenger amenity continued in 1976 when, in pursuit of ever-higher rental income, BR lost the total income from the chemist's shop in February and the loss of the Post Office in March, going the way of the Travelling Post Office, leading to a bizarre omission in a busy commuter station that still had tourist traffic too. Operationally service cuts meant shutting the Windsor/Khartoum Station on Sundays with trains sent to what seemed to us like frontier-territory in Platforms 12 to 15.

In January 1977 the Windsor Tea Room/Windsor Room/The Windsor/Thames Bar complex, which had been empty and disused, a constant irritation to those of us travelling past it (especially after a long trip from Hull via Kings Cross with the tawdry facilities then available there), were surprisingly brought back into use as I discovered on a cold wet day. Alas the former tea room was now a large travel centre, the need for which was not wholly certain, and I recall a crushing disappointment as I arrived for a drink fully aware of

The S15 Class 4-6-0 freight locos entered service on the LSWR in 1920 and ran until 1966. (Les Chatfield)

how I wished to travel to be denied the one and find the other irrelevant. However, in a rather sensitive move by BR, the highly decorative cashier kiosks that Betjeman had waxed so enthusiastically about were retained as attractive display cases for publicity material.

During 1977 all the Bostwick gates, which afforded a clear view of the platform enabling passengers to decide whether to "do a dash for the train" or not, were replaced with a new barrier line. The new barrier line incorporated various shops and kiosks, as indeed WH Smith had at physical intervals between the Bostwick gates, but with the novel twist that the views of the trains were much reduced. Above the new kiosks that obscured the view of trains, Solari departure indicators were erected which were linked to signs at the entrances to the platforms and indeed in various subways. Ironically what could have been a helpful move designed to eliminate the uncertain "dash for the train" was rather under-mined by the fact that these indicators were never as reliable as the mechanical wooden ones installed by the L&SWR which, when they went faulty merely needed a man with a pole to pull things into place! Solari signs were later augmented by dot matrix displays for updates to services; and more recently still the departure signs have been replaced with very efficient screens but which are now fairly standard in any station, a further erosion of station individuality. BR also decided a station name alteration was needed and, on 2nd May 1977, “Waterloo Eastern” simply became “Waterloo East”.

If two stations could have similar names two engines could be named after drawing one man’s funeral train when, on 2nd September 1980, Waterloo was the backdrop for a naming ceremony. The two class 33s that had drawn Mountbatten’s funeral train were named “Earl Mountbatten of Burma “(33. 027); and “The Burma Star” (33.056) in a ceremony at noon.

In October 1980 it was decided commuters needed fast food. BR’s first foray into “fast food” was at Waterloo, with a stunning leap of imagination in this most English of stations serving suburbia, “The Drum” , was named “Casey Jones” after an American railwayman who crashed his locomotive and killed himself thereby failing to reassure many travellers!

The expulsion of Wellington and references to the Napoleonic Wars from Waterloo continued when the Trafalgar Buffet and Bar was remodelled in 1982 becoming The Trips restaurant - its third incarnation in less than ten years. Such culinary restlessness on the part of BR showed much less confidence than the long-enduring Surrey Room with its sole incarnation over half a century!

After 48 years of operation the Waterloo signal box lever frame was replaced by a new NX Panel on February 5th 1984 still located in the same signal box. The signal box changes were not visually obvious from the exterior of this by now iconic guide to the approach to the Waterloo, the sight of which acted as a Pavlovian trigger for the gathering of umbrellas and cases as well as the donning of coats.

Matters were equally challenging for discerning rail travellers at the other end of the station. In 1987 the former toilets for gentlemen opposite Platform 2 were transformed rather ironically into a French bistro which, with even greater irony, closed in 1993 before the first through train from Paris arrived in Waterloo International/Khartoum – at the farthest end of Waterloo from the French styled bistro! Modernisation and refurbishment of the remaining toilets produced a level of corporate blandness and uniformity as well as a shocking increase in the price.

All changes were not debatable however. In common with many old buildings in cities across the country the patina of smokestacks was to be lifted during the eighties with the brickwork and facings along the concourse being cleaned at the turn of the decade and restoring the warm brick colour. In March 1981 a commuting architect felt able to write to Sir Peter Parker, the then Chairman of BR, and praise the introduction of new terrazzo flooring which, while at one with the "corporate design ethos" of the time was a marked improvement on the rather patchy and uneven surface that was extant by then. Terrazzo works, completed in 1983, had the effect of making the station look cleaner and surprisingly more spacious and modern in line with the all-electric ethos first adumbrated so many decades ago by Walker and Drummond.

Also, in common with many large buildings in the eighties, it was decided draughts were fatal and so glazed screening was installed around the Victory Arch in 1980. It was around the same time, having allegedly made it warmer, all the comfortable, wooden benches were removed and replaced with less sleep friendly seating a move justified as a step to reduce vagrants sleeping on the station, but which had unintended consequences. The absence of seats also damaged the time honoured tradition for who had been "up West", especially for those suffering ridiculously early "last late" trains out of Khartoum, kipping until the "milk train". In fact all that happened was vagrants and (would be) "swells" slept on luggage "Brutes" ("British Rail Universal Trolley Equipment", a wheeled platform with a mesh fitted around three sides of the body, and an open fourth side, scrapped in 1999) with the tolerant compliance of railway staff who I fondly recall would often generously supply an early morning cup of "railwaymen's tea".

Beneath the Southern Railway's WW II plaque Railtrack, rather oddly, decided that despite being clearly part of WWII D-Day itself was worthy of commemoration. On 6th June 1994, the fiftieth anniversary of D-Day, Railtrack unveiled a brass plaque commemorating those railwaymen who fell on that day as if they were not included in the Southern Railway's memorial. I saw and regarded all plaques on my trips to Town; it being a source of some sadness that, when I went to look at the station for this book, it was only the sight of me taking pictures seemingly made today's commuters look to see what it was I was photographing.

Lambeth Council also helped travellers and BR by jointly funding, in 1985, improvements to the Colonnade bus stops on Waterloo Road. The Waterloo Road Colonnade and subway, at the north-east side of Waterloo Station which, in a throwback to the pre-Hood improvements, were serviced by rather gloomy stairs and passageways, was a long-neglected part of the station. Lambeth's initiative, in many ways, showed the changed relations from the Lambeth Vestry days between railway and State.

The barber where one could get a cut-throat shave even into the seventies has gone; and the new WH Smith was bright and modern with a "walk in" style rather than the old bookstalls scattered near different sections.

The track layout was changed in the eighties as well. Platforms 1 to 4 were shortened to help rationalise track, while Platforms 9 to 14 had redundant points removed and clearances improved by realigning the track. Track works were linked to the need to replace the now not only obsolete but also time-expired frames and wiring in the 1936 signal box, where the old frames and wiring were replaced by a temporary operating panel. Just as the L&SWR had achieved Herculean signalling works in a small time-frame so BR achieved signalling work during the weekend of 5th February 1984 when a new NX Panel replaced the Westinghouse Frame and controlled a relay room built at the former North side turntable. Government approval to replace all signalling on a like-for-like basis was granted in 1986 as being a pragmatic and cheap alternative – but then Waterloo International was conceived.

CHAPTER NINE

To Waterloo International and beyond

The Class 455 electrical multiple unit has run out of Waterloo on suburban lines since 1982. (Mike Knell)

The ultimate tribute to the design of Hood's Waterloo Station has to be its longevity – almost as great as the pan-European peace that the Battle of Waterloo itself heralded. It was not until the end of the Twentieth Century that, despite all the many changes in services – electrification, loss of porters, loss of the Bournemouth Belle as an all-Pullman service, and nationalisation itself – major infrastructure changes were settled upon at Waterloo. Windsor/Khartoum Station was selected as the location of the new Waterloo International - yet another new name within an existing complex and suggesting that the spectre of top-hatted officials of the L&SWR had not entirely "left the building"! Additionally there was investment to build the Jubilee Line extension on the Tube which would include Waterloo. Predictably, with wonderful Gallic hypocrisy, a Parisian councillor M. Longuepee, protested the new Eurostar terminus would be an affront to French feelings celebrating the battle where Bonaparte was finally defeated, despite Paris hosting Austerlitz Station, named for the battle where Napoleon beat the Russians and Austrians. Furthermore if Mr Blair did not change the name M. Longuepee would campaign to name the Gare du Nord after the Battle of Fontenoy! We can only assume this was a publicity stunt, or that French schooling is lamentable since the Station is not at all named after the battle - but took its name from the bridge (admittedly commemorating the battle).

To sell the idea of Waterloo International and its benefits, an information leaflet was delivered to 85,000 households in Lambeth and parts of Southwark. BR's leaflet stressed extra road traffic could be handled by introducing two way working on the internal BR road system within the station, the Tube had spare capacity, and "The Drain" was already being upgraded with connections at the Bank end giving links to the Docklands Light Railway which served the development area of east London. The new station improvements were to be in a way that "only four small buildings need to be demolished" and that "some 550 jobs will be created for BR staff at the new terminal. Other jobs will be created...by the Customs and Immigration facilities and also the extra shops and catering facilities on the station". BR's press release of 23 January 1987 announced the opening of the new Waterloo International Information Centre, located opposite Platform 21, making the astonishing statement, "that in 2003, ten years after the Channel Tunnel is open, the number of people using Waterloo is still forecast to be below the number who used the station in 1978 ...which also explains why a terminal for Channel Tunnel rail services is needed in central London and why Waterloo has been chosen."

In February BR publicly admitted, with far from atypical inefficiency, they got their figures wrong saying "the error had been made through inadvertent double counting of the number of passengers using the Windsor Line services in 1978". BR stated then that the number of passengers using Waterloo in 1985 had fallen in fact to 48 million from its 1971 peak, "due mainly to firms moving to offices outside central London over the past seven years". Nevertheless BR maintained that Waterloo would still be able to cope with expansion and the projected passenger traffic was expected to rise by between 10 and 13 million by 2003.

Conflict was somewhat evidenced behind the scenes as well as in figures. The BR Investment Committee had concerns about the rising infrastructure costs and did not submit the proposal to the Secretary of State for Transport until February 1990. The Department of Transport were not wholly convinced by the case for Waterloo International and prevaricated, seeking reassurances about project management; causing BR to take the relatively rare step of authorising preliminary work on the scheme before Ministerial consent was granted. Preliminary works for Waterloo International actually began in 1989 with closure of the cab road to increase platform capacity. The original proposals for joint working with P & O came to nothing but Ministerial approval finally came in May 1990, the project being priced at some £100 million over four levels: car park (basement), customs and immigration, departures / arrivals, and platforms.

Nicholas Grimshaw and Partners were selected to design the new terminal within a terminus and thereby sweep away the old Khartoum with more courage than the L&SWR but with no more overall harmony to the design. Khartoum was an operating province of Network South East and clearly they, as well as their passengers, would need relocating, which was where BR's foresight in acting before their consent came into its own. On the site of the dock sidings and the vehicular roadway between Platforms 11 and 12 a long platform with two faces had been built which came into use on 2nd July 1990 being then numbered 12 and 13; with the existing Platforms 12 to 15 renumbered as 14 to 17.

The Waterloo signal box was also closed with the entrance-exit panel being moved to a temporary box the iconic 1936 signal box finally closed on 30th October 1990. To facilitate Waterloo International the panel/temp box finally closed on 21st April 1991 when control of Waterloo Station passed to the Wimbledon Signal Centre at Wimbledon, thereby ending some 143 years of signalling control being at Waterloo. Another "victim" of the remodelling required for the Waterloo International was the hoist that had serviced "The Drain" and, in October 1990, to those who knew where to look for it and what it did this engineering symbol was removed from the "station-scene".

Network South East obtained two shorter platforms (18 and 19) at the outer end of "The Village" on 3rd December 1990 allowing the rest of Khartoum to be handed over for "redevelopment". On completion of the works Platforms 18 and 19 would be extended to full-length and connect to the concourse directly. "The Village", that unintended consequence of the creation of the new modern station, was cleared and the stationmaster, as well as others, placed on a raft above Platforms 1 to10 (another bizarre successor to the former loco-men's raft above Platforms 1 to 6).

Time, tide, and demolition men wait for no-man and the demolition of the 1885 Khartoum station started, at the supporting brick arches, when the then Minister for Public Transport, Roger Freeman, on 11th December 1990 ceremonially used a pneumatic drill on the station. The later demolition of "The Village" block allowed the insertion of two more platform faces underneath the roof of the main station.

Foundations of the terminal were deemed complete by July 1991 allowing superstructure works to commence.

Further down the station more indignities were heaped on the former Surrey Room: with headquarters staff moved away from the station to an office block in the Blackfriars Road the former elegant rooms became part of a high-level walkway in January 1993. With heavy road traffic expected for the new station, and vehicular movement considered a priority, it was decided to dispense with the pedestrian crossing that had linked the two former L&SWR and SER stations, lifts/escalators and stairs from concourse level sweeping people through the Surrey Room on a high-level walkway instead.

Waterloo International was completed and handed over to the operator, three years to the month after gaining approval, on 17th May 1993 with much publicity about it being on time and on budget. However the fact was that by May the following year the final cost was given as £145,000,000 which was in fact £48, 000,000 above what the Secretary of State had authorised and international passenger services did not commence operation until 14th November 1994 because of delays to the completion of the Channel Tunnel.

Intended as an homage in steel and glass to the traditional train shed Waterloo International has an elegance of curve that belies the increasingly run down and dated pedestrian approaches to the former Khartoum. The station has 36 structural bays where, a flattened bow string arch of three pins has the "central" of the three moved to a side because of the undulating height from east to west. The western-most truss is shorter and rises steeply because the station boundary is so close to the track, whilst the longer truss spanning the other tracks rises more gently. Each roof truss is stabilised by a tension rod, running above the shorter truss and under the longer one like a bow-string. Extending for the length of the beautifully styled sleek double-length Eurostar trains access to railway modernity was again facilitated by the foresight of the L&SWR. By removing the original concourse level thereby opening the arch level "to the skies" and demolishing the arches more space was created.

Railwaymen are railwaymen whether L&SWR or BR and this area was soon dubbed the orchestra pit. With the arrivals hall, departure lounge and check-in all on the ground floor they were connected to the original station level, where the platforms remained, by angled travolators. The design of the station was arguably marred by the treatment of passenger facilities where many feel it is a mistake to adopt the air-terminal technique of hoarding passengers into an impersonal waiting area, before they are allowed to board the train but the station roof was a welcome return to the Victorian concept of vaulted station roofs being the first clear span terminus to be built in London since St Pancras in 1868, and something not hitherto a feature readily associated with Waterloo Station.

The Government of the day was of the opinion railways could neither expand or be adequately maintained when limited by the many demands on the public purse. As a prelude to privatisation therefore the domestic station became part of Railtrack on 1st April 1994 and during privatisation, floated on the London Stock Exchange on 20th May 1996, whilst Waterloo International station was transferred to London & Continental Railways, with a book value of £136 million.

All new developments at Waterloo were not necessarily above platforms, nor necessarily operational. In 1997 the artist Mike Rundall unveiled his sculpture which, chameleon-like, changed colour to mirror the people standing around it in the concourse at Waterloo, near the departing Eurostar trains. The sculpture, also broadcasted snatches of radio from around the world in a manner reminiscent of the Tower of Babel.

The 1999 extension to the underground's Jubilee Line, placing Waterloo between Westminster and Southwark stations, also owed much to the foresight of the L&SWR in building high. The Jubilee Line booking hall occupied the former Waterloo Road entrance that had hitherto been an omnibus station at the north-eastern corner of the station, the area known as The Colonnades. New escalators to the Jubilee Line platforms below and also the main-line concourse above, whilst introducing a travolator in a deep tube tunnel to the Bakerloo and Northern Line under the York Road end of the station meant no major intervention in the main-line station was needed – a considerable boon when handling in excess of 90 million passenger movements a year.

Despite Waterloo International being a very modern addition featuring an up to the minute bolted glass roof, the Waterloo Station roof was in a sorry state of repair and starting to "tire". Over the years, repairs had inevitably been carried out but on an ad-hoc basis creating a patchwork of different glass, various glazing bars and even

In 1996 Richard Branson launched the Virgin/Eurostar train direct to Disneyland Paris

'temporary' timber panels which had long ago been overlooked for replacement. Work started in August 2001 on a £36 ½ million pound refurbishment scheme with Morgan Sindall appointed the design and build contractor, responsible for all elements of the design, procurement, project management.

Fortunately, the roof's original steelwork remained in good condition despite being in need of blasting & repainting but still required McNealty Brown, of Prentis Quay, Sittingbourne to dismantle and remove, the original wrought steel trusses from Waterloo's roof. The steel trusses were then repaired, refurbished, galvanised, returned to Waterloo and re-fitted in their original locations with new galvanised steel purlins fitted between to take the new roofing system. However because the roof's spans varied in size a flexible roofing system was essential to accommodate the tolerance and variance of the site conditions. A system was found, supplied by the Lonsdale Metal Company Ltd using their SkyGard product, and installed by Kelsey

Roofing Industries Ltd. Despite SkyGard being a tried and tested product, specially extended fixing brackets had to be developed to permit ventilation at the bottom of each tier of glazing thereby allowing air-circulation so diesel exhaust, carrying with it dirt & grime detrimental to the to the glass and aluminium system, could escape whilst still preventing undue rainwater penetration. Despite considering polyester powder paint finish a mill finish option was selected thereby saving millions of pounds because a painted finish required regular cleaning to maintain warranty agreements – a warranty that 25 years would be maintenance free within the estimated 75 year life-span of the new roof. To complete the installation 1/4 " laminated glass was fitted, this being specially cut to size by The Dorset Glass Company, Poole using state of the art computer aided machinery.

The work was completed in March 2003, a stupendous achievement over 25 months replacing almost 25,000 panes of glass on some 33,500 square yards of roof. During the roof-works opportunity was taken to install new structural galvanised gutters with walkways to replace the existing provision as well as works to the South, West, and North elevations of the building to provide the steel support needed for new glazing and walkways, and the renewal of the steel works to the platform canopies was also included for a further £800,000. The roof replacement was a significant achievement and a necessary form of working given that between 2002 and 2003 68,432,000 people used the station, a station which in 2002 passed from the ownership of Railtrack to Network Rail.

Thirteen years after opening, with none of the longevity accorded to any of its predecessors on site, and despite year on year increases in passenger numbers Waterloo International was no more. As predicted the high speed Euro-star trains sharing the approach roads with "third-rail pick-up" suburban commuter trains et al did not work. Indeed when Eurostar services first began, Waterloo International had only eight pathways in and out, split between trains to and from Paris and Brussels. When, in 1998, the decision was taken to build the new high speed line, HS1, it was perhaps inevitable that it would run through Kent – one of the eastern Home Counties. By building the line under the Thames and through the east end of London it made operational sense, if no nod to history and romance, to site the new terminus at St Pancras. In November 2007 the new Eurostar terminal at St Pancras was opened and Waterloo International was mothballed on the 13th of that month. Whilst consideration was given to keeping Waterloo International active and operating approximately a third of Eurostar trains from there the cost of maintaining two station hubs was deemed too great. It was also decided, in 2008, that Waterloo International would transfer from London & Continental Railways to the Government, in exchange for the new maintenance depot at Temple Mills in East London, and be managed by BRB (Residual) Ltd.

A return to use for Platform 20 was expected when it was converted for use by domestic trains in 2008 – the then Parliamentary Under-Secretary of State for Transport, Paul Clark, saying in November 2008 that the cost of the conversion works at Platform 20 was "in the region of £2.9 million". The money was spent installing signs, electronic departure boards, and creating holes in the wall between Platform 19 in the domestic station and Platform 20 in the former International terminal, effectively the other half of domestic Platform 19, to improve access from the main concourse. Excited commuters expecting some easing of congestion were to be disappointed because the new facilities were not brought into use. South West Trains ran the first test train into Platform 20 on 4th June 2008, to aid driver training but it remains closed.

In fairness it is more than just the station that needs works to make it operational. As in the case going back to the days of Chaplin operability depends on access and to convert Waterloo International to domestic operation requires the demolition of the earlier Nine Elms Flyover, linking the station to the "Chatham" main line. A Government Report concluded that sufficient capacity to run scheduled services over this connection was not available, because the double-track viaduct only accommodated a maximum of eight trains an hour. The lengthy International station platforms also require raising, because they were constructed to the lower European profile, something which had no doubt made sense at the time they were built.

Away from Waterloo International the curse of the automatic (non-functioning) ticket barrier finally arrived at Waterloo in June 2008. A row of squat plastic pods not guaranteed to cope with one person at a time, unlike Bostwick gates which at least permitted flexibility to cope with varying crowd demands and had some aesthetic value, as well as allowing a passenger focussed service. By removing the personnel, as a cost-cutting measure, the operational needs of the railway were put before the passengers at this the busiest station in the country, despite some attempts to promote it as an aesthetic improvement again allowing a return to being able to see the platforms. The automated barrier scheme saw a staggering 117 automatic gates constructed at the entrances to the platforms and in the subway (the figure was later given as increasing to 130 on the concourse and 27 in the subway). At the same period the inevitable modern CCTV cameras arrived, 118 of them and a CCTV control room, with related electrical works throughout the station. These works were executed by Murphy, Bailey Rail, and AM Security Services

The continuing debacle of redundant station platforms at the busiest station in the UK was in no way addressed when, in February 2010, The Old Vic acquired a new performance space beneath Waterloo Station. Acquired from BRB (Residuary) Ltd, the Government-owned firm responsible for the station, The Old Vic media release claimed, "This unique venue showcases productions, performances and installations and will continue to be home to a series of innovative and surprising arts events throughout 2011/12."

The Queen of Jordan was one of 800 guests at the ARK fundraising dinner held at Waterloo International on Thursday night 13th May 2010. Hosted by ARK founder Arpad Busson and his girlfriend Uma Thurman the dinner included Michael Gove, Kevin Spacey, Lord Levy, Naomi Campbell, Eva Herzigova and Tessa Dahl as guests, some paying £10,000 a head, and raffle tickets selling for £5,000. A Fiat 500 painted by Damien Hirst was auctioned for

£90,000 and the party raised just over £14 million in the second year that ARK used Waterloo's disused Eurostar terminal as the venue for its party.

Back in the real world a desire to modernise Waterloo was revealed with the announcement, in November 2010, of a proposal to erect a new retail balcony.

If, at Waterloo Station, offices could be adapted to shops then, in December 2010, the versatile station complex could adapt to a new form of commuting – the bicycle. Located in the immediate vicinity of Waterloo the station had also, by now, provided cycle storage accommodation, designed to accommodate 124 bicycles on the European model, just a little further down on Station Approach. Boris Bikes were also introduced conveniently located just outside the station. Plus ca change: commuters complain that Boris Bikes are depleted often as early as 8 a.m., and there are insufficient spaces in the other racks. However since the scheme launched new docks have been installed and extended around Waterloo. More significantly, to facilitate extra bikes during peak times, a storage cage area in Waterloo Station has been installed, rather amusingly on the former connecting bridge to the SER line thereby finding a modern transport use for a failed transport link. The end result is a much improved experience on the original situation although it is still difficult despite the Boris Bike concept not being planned around peak hour travel at commuter termini. Indeed in a short video, reported on 19th September, 2012, City University London used data from the first 5 million trips made by cyclists in the Boris Bike scheme, which itself had launched in July 2010. The resulting map perhaps unsurprisingly showed three commuter hot spots: Waterloo Station and the City's financial district in the east, in and out of King's Cross and St. Pancras stations in the north, as well as around and through Hyde Park in the west.

The weekend of 17th September 2011 saw the station host Top Shop's catwalk show as part of London Fashion Week and a rather defensive BRB (Residual) publicise that events in the building have raised almost £30 million for children's charities much of that total accounted for by the two Ark charity balls.

CHAPTER TEN

The latest reboot

In 2011 it was revealed that it had cost taxpayers over £4 million to keep the platforms at Waterloo International Station closed which was clearly an untenable position in the country's busiest station. Indeed a study by the Office of Rail Regulation, released on 2nd April 2012, put the number of people entering and exiting Waterloo Station for April 2010 to March 2011 at 91,750, 382, a 6.2%

The main concourse seen from the southern end of the new balcony in October 2012.

161

rise (over 5 million more passenger entries and exits) on the figures for the previous year. Furthermore the retail sector was no longer so antipathetic to station trading. Indeed across the whole operation Network Rail reported a 3.85% rise in sales for the three months ending on 30th September 2011, driven by strong growth across its food and beverage categories. During the period compared against the previous year: Bars reported growth of 10.4 %, specialist food retailers 10.2 percent and restaurants 6.78 %

With such figures it was perhaps not surprising that, just over a century after the first above ground visible works of the new station materialised there was again a new debate about Waterloo – or was it really a new debate? Discussions between those charged with operating Waterloo reflected many recurrent themes: to fill the concourse or not, to overhaul the station or modernise it to reflect contemporary needs within the constraints of a substantial existing building, and the ever present need to earn an income. Decisions were made however but in different climates to those experienced by BR. The dead hand of the Treasury was no longer omnipresent, and so the Waterloo concept in station trading began with a decision to clear the concourse, use modern materials to build a mezzanine floor and, plus ca change, improve the connections to Waterloo East with work on the balcony starting in April 2011.

Such dynamism within Network rail was countered by BRB (Residuary) Limited at the mothballed Waterloo International Station. With the expectations of new suburban rolling stock arriving at a reopened Platform 20 instead Waterloo International saw an 1870 crack express arrive – for "The Railway Children" featuring a Great Northern locomotive, Patrick Stirling's 8' single "No.1", an engine with no connection to the LNER of the area of the novel or the L&SWR venue of the play! With previews from: 18 June 2011, the highly successful and well received play ended its second season on 8 January 2012, having had an equally successful first season from 4th July to 4th September 2010

Justine Greening, the Secretary of State for Transport, on 23rd December 2011 announced that Platform 20 of the former Eurostar terminal, which had been worked on three years earlier, would be opened in 2014. The extra platform was required because the Government had decided to provide funding to South West Trains so they could lease 50 extra carriages and provide longer peak-hour trains with extra services on the Reading line thereby providing capacity for some 8,000 extra peak-time passengers. It was expected the extra trains, refurbished class 460 'Juniper' units formerly used by Gatwick Express, would start to enter service from May 2013, with all the units in place by July 2014.

Concern about the wasted potential of Waterloo was not confined to Ministerial circles. With platform occupancy in the morning rush hour at Euston and Paddington being a problem and a review of sleeper-trains underway rail sleeper-service enthusiasts suggested, in March 2012, the creation of a new franchise, solely operating sleeper-trains, exclusively using Waterloo International. Surprisingly Waterloo International is actually quite easily accessible from Scotland via Kensington Olympia and from the Great Western via Acton and also has sufficient long platforms available. Although a sleeper may have had a slim chance it was probably never going to be viable since growth figures for Waterloo suggest what has been evident for its entire history – all space was needed for commuters. Network Rail commented that with over 90 million passengers passing through Waterloo every year and a 30 % growth in passenger transport predicted by 2030; coupled with the imminent London 2012 Olympics the clear challenge for the Network Rail/South West Trains alliance was delivering extra capacity ensuring passengers got reliable rail services.

On 30th April 2012, for the first time since privatisation, a single executive team to manage rolling stock and the track was formed when Stagecoach and Network Rail made a deal, to run the railway under a single structure on the South West Trains network intended to operate until Stagecoach's franchise agreement for South West Trains ends in 2017. The first concrete action was to combine the two management teams at Waterloo Station into a single unit. Network Rail Chief Executive David Higgins claiming the move was part of a drive to devolve decision making from the centre and towards "front-line managers". Managing director Tim Shoveller, Managing Director of South West Trains, headed the combined management structure, led by nine executives grandiloquently called the "Alliance Senior Management Team".

With four new escalators and lifts, opening on 29th May 2012, Waterloo Station acquired step-free access to Waterloo East. The works also marked the first stage of the balcony completion, and exposed the earlier abolition of the Surrey Room features.

By June 2012 the Waterloo Control Centre had recognised what was happening unofficially with some staff on South West Trains and was running an official twitter account from the busy Waterloo Control Centre. Whilst the railways may readily admit they were not in the forefront of embracing the new technology, the fact that the social media and digital communications exist is only a logical extension of the use of loudspeakers.

With the imminent arrival of the Olympics and an anticipated extra demand at Waterloo of another 80,000 passengers a day, it was announced in June 2012 that "The Drain"—was to open on Sundays throughout the Games renewing Sunday services which had last operated regularly between 1943 and 1947. "The Drain" supplied a critical link for spectators being a direct access to the Docklands Light Railway and Central line at Bank avoiding the Jubilee line. "The Drain" also helped people to avoid London Bridge, which was already being forecast to be one of the most overcrowded stations throughout the entire Games.

In July 2012 Justine Greening's attention again returned to Waterloo when she announced a £350 million plan to extend platforms at that Station. The proposal formed part of the "High Level Output Specification" programme (as modern management-corporate-political speak demands) for 2014-2019 published by the Department for Transport. The platform lengthening project was part of a series of measures intended to create extra capacity for commuters into London by running longer trains. Department for Transport estimates are predicated on the belief that the number of

Singer Rihanna used Waterloo to attend the concert of Drake at the O2 in March 2012. (Liam Mendes)

passengers arriving at Waterloo during the three busiest hours of the morning rush "hour" is likely to increase by nearly 10% between 2012-17. It was perhaps therefore no surprise that South West Trains in July also announced that from May 2013 trains extended from eight to 10 carriages will leave Windsor, easing pressure on stations further up the line at Staines, Twickenham and Richmond. Furthermore commuters travelling on the Waterloo-bound line from Reading after May 2013 would from 2014 also begin "benefiting" from two extra rush-hour trains - at the extraordinarily uncivilised times of 6.24am and 6.54am.

Customer needs were also being attended to in the "here and now" when, on 17th July 2012, the new balcony, just over 240 yards long, opened at Waterloo after little more than a year of works. The greatest length of any such undertaking at any British railway station the project was part of Network Rail's £25 million improvement project to transform the station and smooth the journey for the

300,000 passengers who passed through each day. By installing escalators, and repositioning retail outlets previously located in the middle of the main concourse onto the balcony congestion was considerably eased The balcony was built by BAM Construct UK Limited with all the architectural metalwork for the aluminium cladding, main staircases and stainless steelwork for the shops being undertaken by Mercia Architectural Ltd of Dudley. Cape Electrical & Mechanical Ltd of Romford Essex carried out the mechanical and electrical works to the existing and remaining Network Rail offices on the second third and fourth floors of the Office block meaning six new service risers had to be built by BAM Construction.

Network Rail's rejuvenation of Waterloo was part of a programme of investment in key stations across the country intended to provide more space, reduce congestion and improve the facilities for passengers in a return to the concept of customer care. The political premise underpinning the privatisation had been Networks Rail's retail and commercial activities should generate funds for reinvestment directly back into the railway so limiting costs to taxpayers.

As Barry Norman never actually said: "and why not?" Waterloo, as both the L&SWR (after the initial years) and the Southern knew, is a very busy station and ever more so. Removing retail units from the concourse by opening the balcony, whatever the debate about ruination of the aesthetic merits and intent of the original station planners reduced congestion but still provided the facilities expected at a modern station and made it easier to get to and from the core business: the train services.

The new balcony provided passengers with a wider choice of places to eat and shop. This new retail expansion encouraged new brands such as Yo! Sushi, Fat Face, Hotel Chocolat, Oliver Bonas, Links of London, Thomas Pink, Carluccio's, Kiehl's Sports Bar & Grill, Benugo and Corney & Barrow's new concept bar The Cabin, with new-to-station brand Joules. In total all the new units gave a retail capacity within the station totalling 55,000 sq ft across 38 stores.

Having consolidated the retail offer the next crucial stage for

Waterloo was to extend the platforms and run longer trains with more capacity, to cater for the predicted growth in passenger numbers. Over the last few weeks of August 2012 engineering work on the lines and canopy of the former Khartoum/Windsor/Waterloo International was started, the roof repairs undertaken by Walker Construction who had been appointed by BRB (Residual) in May 2012. The engineering works were clearly visible and comprehensible on the cleaned and repainted roof with passengers still expecting that one of the platforms will be used by domestic trains from 2014 but there is still no formal announcement of the future use of the other former platforms at Waterloo International terminal.

As a pioneer in loudspeakers it is fitting that Waterloo is trying again to get it right with works starting in August 2012 and expected to be completed by early 2013 despite the "acoustically challenging" environment. The South West Trains/Network Rail Alliance is funding £2.8m to provide clearer announcements for some 350, 000 passengers per day. The new system produces 90 decibels of sound in an emergency to be heard over the crowds and is connected to almost 1,000 speakers around the station. The first phase of the new system went live in the main concourse and new balcony before the start of the 2012 Olympic Games. However it was noticeable, whilst sitting sipping a cocktail on a Sunday in October 2012 as part of the less arduous researches for this book, that it was possible to count more CCTV cameras than (sometimes rather dusty) existing loudspeakers. NG Bailey Rail Division was awarded a £2.5m contract by Network Rail to replace the loudspeaker system at Waterloo Station with the very latest in speaker technology, and one that also met stringent new fire compliance standards. As ever in works at this busy station throughout the project, Waterloo had to remain fully operational, meaning there were no on-site storage facilities and engineers had just three hours a day in which to install the equipment. Chris Raven, managing director of NG Bailey Rail Division, said: "The new system provides a modern standard of crystal-clear sound cover for the whole station, and spells the end of the days under the former system when announcements reverberated around the station." However having a sandwich on the new balcony the new system may not reverberate but it was also barely audible on 2nd December 2012 despite being better on the concourse itself.

Whatever the audibility of loudspeakers, the sheer volume of travelers in Waterloo makes it an ideal venue for promotional offers as when, on 31st August 2012, promotional staff gave away free Strawberry Mivvi Ice Lollies, the strawberry ice lolly with ice cream in the middle, the company clearly regarding hot commuters in a specific target group as ideal in helping the lolly make a bit of a

Empty tracks at Waterloo in 1989 as a strike by ASLEF brought the train system to a halt.

comeback. Indeed on-station sales were a growth sector with retail sales results for the three months to 30th September 2012 growing by 2.37% compared to the same period in 2011, against high street sales only growing by 0.05%.

In September 2012 informal eco-proposals after an American model were made for the rail bridge over Waterloo Road the bridge which once carried the railway linking the platforms at Waterloo Station with the Charing Cross – London Bridge line. New York's High Line is one of their most successful urban redevelopment projects; a mile-long section of a former elevated freight railway mothballed in the 1980s and re-opened in 2009 as an urban park. Between 5th and 8th October 2012 the High Line Symposium at the Garden Museum was held. The American project's founders visited London and discussed how they brought it to fruition. Boris Johnson, as Mayor of London, supported A High Line for London: Green Infrastructure Ideas for a New London Landscape part of the Landscape Institute's Green Infrastructure competitions as part of the Symposium. The Mayor's office said they would run an open competition to "design innovative new places that enrich London's Infrastructure" which was not intended to merely replicate the High Line.

Within the general symposium framework The Land Trust and Free Architecture also entered a proposal to turn the mothballed Waterloo International Station into a green space. Requiring no structural change to Grimshaw's structure the proposals were for 99 railway carriages parked along the platforms accommodating a farmers' market. The station itself would house street food stalls, incubator units, design studios, cinemas, lecture halls and small retail spaces with allotments; all within the station space described as a "ready-made greenhouse", thereby providing "an English country garden in the city all year round." The judges chose not to shortlist the rus in urbe scheme perhaps aware that Network Rail planned to re-open the first of the disused platforms in 2014.

Environmentally friendly themes continued when, on Wednesday 31st October 2012, there was a celebratory opening party at the new

Lush store on Waterloo Station Concourse (opposite Platform 1). What was described as a 'New Concept' shop design, central to which was a country kitchen table consultation area where customers sit and discuss their skincare needs with consultants. The new look really takes things 'back to basics', with a simplicity to the design, and clean lines that highlight the products, rather than compete with them, in some ways and no doubt unconsciously harking back to the relatively clean and simple lines of the station building on the concourse itself.

Wandsworth Council, in December 2012, informed me they were stepping back from Airtrack-lite in favour of the "South London-Heathrow Rail link" Proposal. With Surrey conducting a rail study, Wandsworth are considering a parallel study to consider route options with a workshop for interested parties taking place on 27th February 2013 intending to inform a consultancy for three months from March at a cost of £25,000 which, with my patient publisher pressing for a manuscript in early 2013 seems a good place to stop. After a lifetime of public service I have learned to dread the phrase "feasibility study" and even more when conjoined with "consultant" but recognize the realpolitik of Wandsworth's approach and hope they succeed. In 1848 the L&SWR just built a railway line and station after parliamentary approval. In the early Twentieth Century the railway needed parliamentary approval, to placate two tiers of councils, assuage competing railway interests, and deal with sometimes self-appointed interest groups. By the early Twenty-first Century there are so many lobby groups, focused often around the most micro of interests that preparatory work to even think of a new option for Waterloo needs endless consultation! Watch this space!

Financial planning is as speculative and uncertain as route planning. As of closing for publication the historical continuum seems to reflect another expansionary cycle is beginning. Network Rail's Strategic Business Plan for the five years from 2014-19, published in January 2013, discusses post 2019 growth options. The almost perennial L&SWR attention to the approaches is a strand in the Plan mentions "consideration of land take in the Waterloo area to improve the approaches into the station" as a possibility for Network Rail to help meet the passenger growth projections by 2031. Tim Shoveller, no doubt reflecting the Government announcement of increased funding being imminent comments, "More passengers create a need for more trains which places an even greater demand on an aging infrastructure which is 175 years old in parts. We will be investing heavily in increasing the network's resilience and reliability and doing everything we can to be able to provide a railway which can accommodate the extra trains needed to cope with growing demand." The ghosts of Atkinson's Trustees must be whispering into speculator's ears as we speak and by the time Network Rail are ready to act they should find land in hostile and speculative hands!

REFERENCES

Some works I have used, excluding novels etc, and which I thought informative include:-

Allen, Cecil J *Salute to the Southern*
Ian Allan London 1974

Barker, T.C. & Robbins M *A history of London Transport, passenger travel and the development of the metropolis vol 1 the Nineteenth* Century Allen & Unwin 1963

Betjeman, John, *London's Historic Railway Stations*
John Murray London 1972

British Rail Board *Facts and Figures about British Rail*
BR London 1967

British Transport Commission *Facts and Figures about British Rail*
BTC London 1959

Broadbridge, Samuel *Studies in Railway Expansion and the Capital Market in England 1825 – 1873*
Frank Cass London 1970

Carter, Ernest F *An Historical Geography of the Railways of the British Isles*
Cassell London 1959

Chivers, Colin & Wood, Philip *Waterloo Station circa 1900*
South Western Circle Monograph 3 2006

Clarke, John *The Brookwood Necropolis Railway"*
Oakwood Press 4th edition Usk 2006

Cleveland-Stevens, Edward *English Railways, their development and their relation to the State*
George Routledge and Sons Limited London 1915

Conder, Francis Roubiliac (ed Jack Simmons) *The Men Who Built Railways*
Thomas Telford Limited London 1983 (This is a reprint of the Author's *"Personal recollections of English Engineers")*

Darwin, Bernard *War on the Line, the story of the Southern Railway in war-time*
The Southern Railway Company London 1946

Dendy Marshall, C. F. *History of The Southern Railway*
Ian Allan Shepperton 1968
Ellis, Claude Hamilton *Four Main Lines*
George Allen & Unwin London 1950
Ellis, Claude Hamilton *The South Western Railway, its mechanical history and background 1838-1922*
George Allen and Unwin Ltd London 1956
Emmerson, Andrew *Discovering Subterranean London*
Shire Publications Oxford 2010
Evans, AKB & Gough, JV (ed) *The Impact of the Railway on Society in Britain, essays in honour of Jack Simmons*
Ashgate Aldershot 2003
Faulkner, J. N. & Williams, R. A. *The London and South Western Railway in the 20th Century*
David & Charles Newton Abbot 1988
Findlay George *The working and Management of an English Railway*
Whittaker & Co 4th edition London 1891
Freeman, Roger & Shaw, Jon *All Change British Railway Privatisation*
McGraw Hill Publishing Maidenhead 2000
Gibb, Richard (ed) *The Channel Tunnel, a geographical perspective*
John Wiley and Sons Chichester 1994
Gillam, John C *The Waterloo and City Railway*
Oakwood Press Monmouth 2001
Gouvish, Terry *British Railways 1948-1973 A Business History*
Cambridge 1986
Gouvish, Terry *British Railways 1974 – 1997 From Integration to privatisation*
Oxford 2002
Green, Oliver *Discovering London Railway Stations*
Shire Oxford 2011
Hadley A.T. *Railroad Transportation* 1886
Jackson, Alan A & Croome, Desmond F *Rails through the Clay, a history of London's tube railways*
George Allen & Unwin London 1962
Jackson, Alan A *London's Termini*
David and Charles Newton Abbot 2nd edition 1985
Jerome, Jerome K *Three Men in a Boat, (to say nothing of the dog)*
Alan Sutton 1989 original edition 1889

Kellet, John R *The Impact of Railways on Victorian Cities*
Routledge and Kegan Paul London 1969

L&SWR *Timetable as posted on Queens Road Battersby* 1870

L&SWR *Timetable as posted on Queens Road Battersby* 1879

L&SWR Railway (Henry Holmes Office of Superintendent of the Line) *Instructions To All Concerned As To The Working Of The Waterloo And City Railway*
Waterlow & Sons Limited London issued 15th October 1903

L&SWR Railway, *The Opening of The New Station Waterloo*
London 1922

Morgan, Bryn (ed) *The Railway Lovers Companion*
Eyre and Spottiswoode London 1963

Nock, O.S. *Railway Centenary 1825-1925 supplement to the Locomotive, Railway carriage & Wagon review* London 1925

Nock, O.S. *The London & South Western Railway*
Ian Allen Shepperton 1971

Nock, O.S. *"Railway Reminiscences of the Interwar years*
Ian Allen Shepperton 1990

Ottley, George A *Bibliography of Railway History* HMSO 1983

Railway Gazette *Waterloo Station Rebuilding*

Railway Gazette *The New Waterloo Station*
reprint from Railway Gazette 9th June 1922

Reed, M.C. *Investment in Railways in Britain 1820-1844, a study in the development of the capital market*
Oxford University Press London 1975

Reilly, Charles *Some Architectural problems of Today* 1924

Richards, Jeffrey and MacKenzie, John M *The Railway Station, a social history*
Oxford 1986

Richardson, R.C. *The Broad Gauge and the Narrow Gauge Railways and Religion in Victorian England*
NEED MORE DETAILS

Roberts, Sir Howard & Godfrey, Walter (eds) *"London County Council Survey of London,*
South Bank and Vauxhall, the Parish of St Mary Lambeth Part I vol XXIII LCC London 1951

Ruskin, John (ed Cook E.T. & Wedderburn A) *The Seven lamps of Architecture*
1903-1912 vol viii

Sherrington, C.E.R. *Economics of Rail Transport in Great Britain*
Edward Arnold London`1928

Simmons, Jack *The Railways of Britain, an historical introduction*
Routledge & Kegan Paul London 1961

Simmons, Jack *The Railways of Britain, a journey through history*
Guild London 1986

Simmons, Jack *The Railway in Town and Country 1830-1914*
David and Charles Newton Abbott 1986

Simmons, Jack & Biddle, Gordon (eds) *Oxford Companion to British Railway History*
Oxford 1997

Szlumper, Alfred Weeks *The Signalling at the Waterloo Terminus of the London and South-Western Railway*
Institute of Civil Engineers Minutes of the Proceedings,Volume 111 Issue 1893 01 January 1893 pages231 –256

Tiresarias (Roger Green) *Notes from Overground* 1984

Whitbread, J.R. *The Railway Policeman*
George Harrap London 1961

White, H.P. *A Regional History of the Railways of Great Britain Vol 2*
David and Charles 2nd edition Dawlish 1964

Williams, R. A. *The London & South Western Railway, Vol 1: The Formative Years, Vol 2: Growth and Consolidation*
David and Charles Newton Abbott 1968

Wolmar Christian *Fire and Steam a new History of the Railways in Britain*
Allantic London 2007

Bretwalda Books Ltd